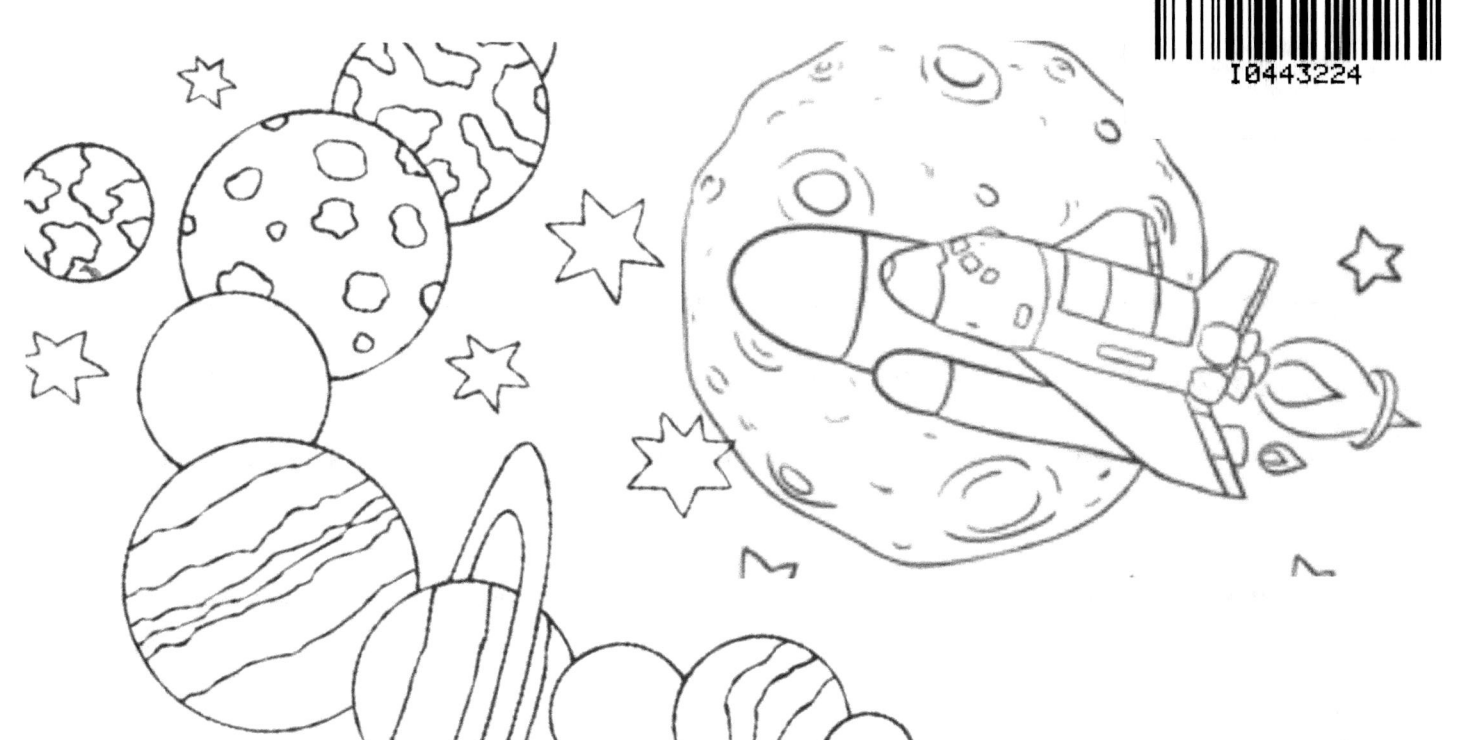

SPACE COLORING BOOK

For Kids

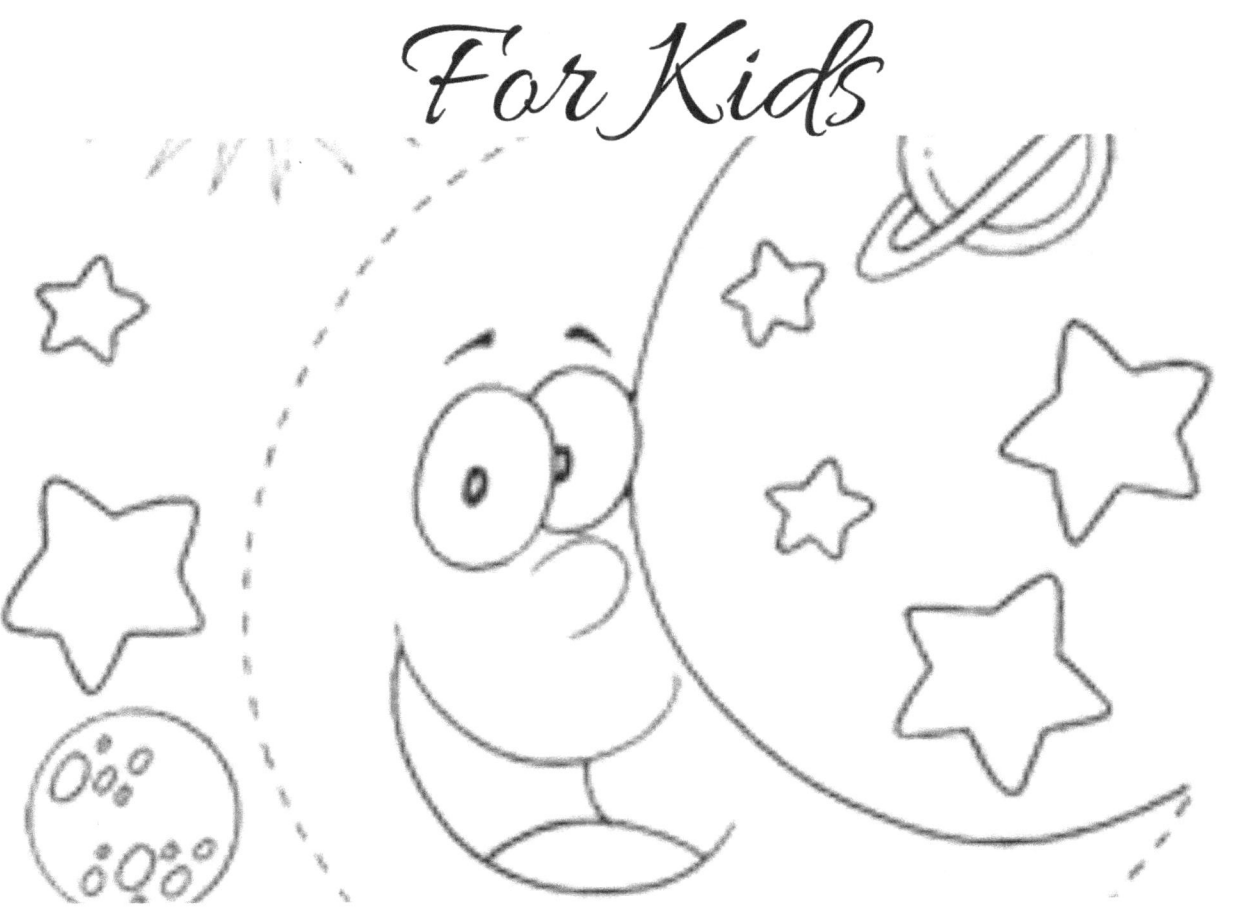

Space Coloring Book for Kids

Fantastic Outer Space Coloring with Planets, Astronauts, Space Ships, Rockets

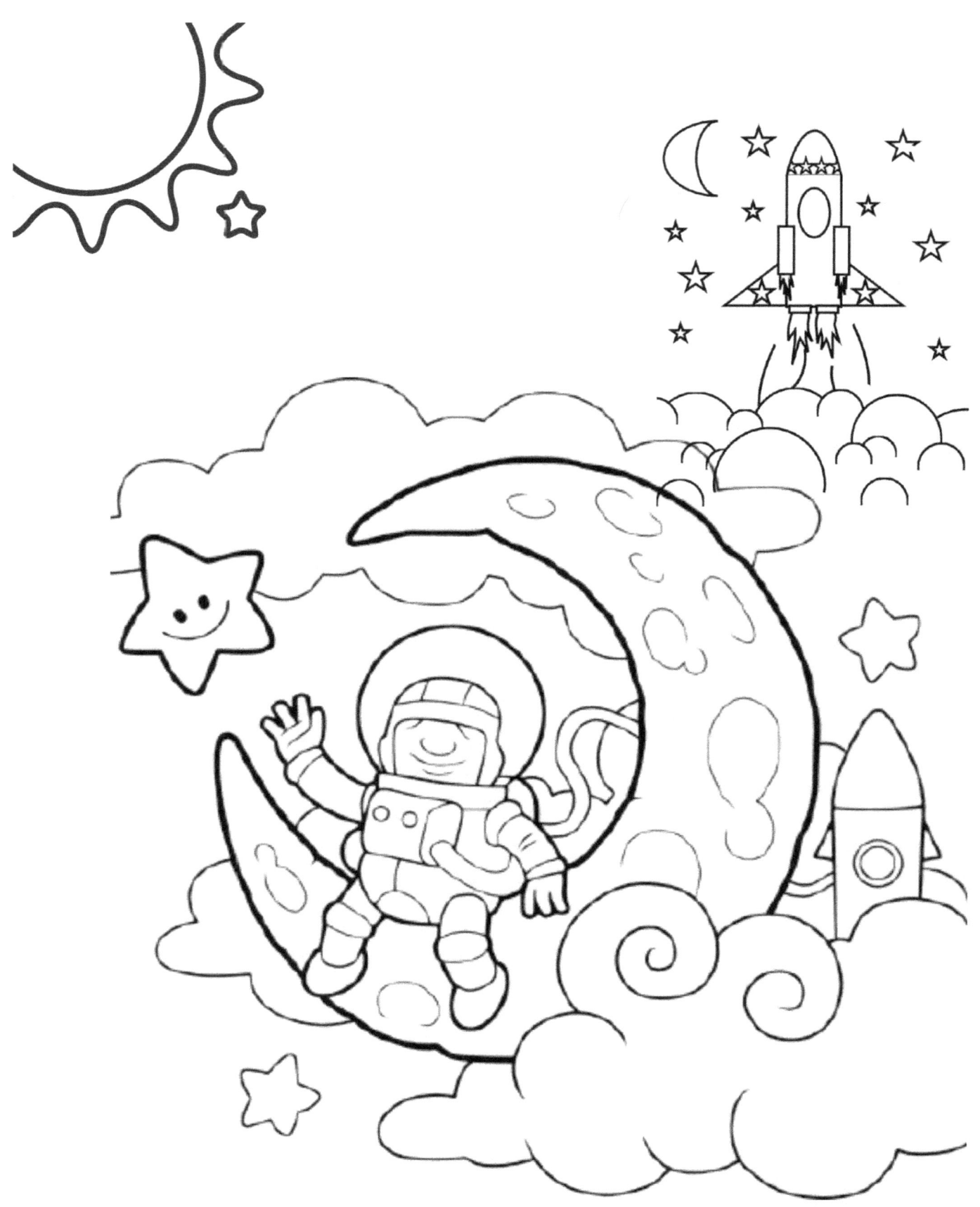

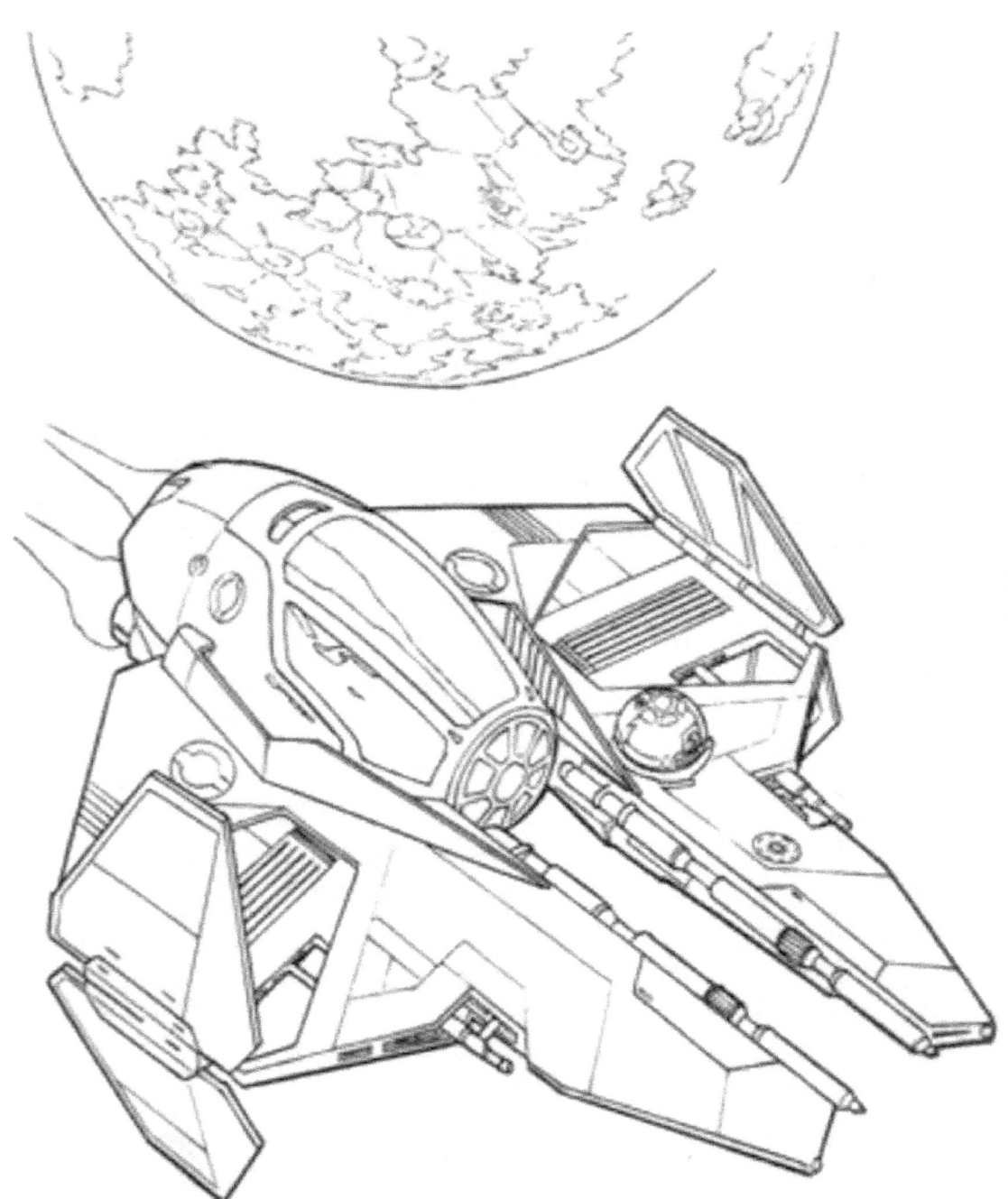

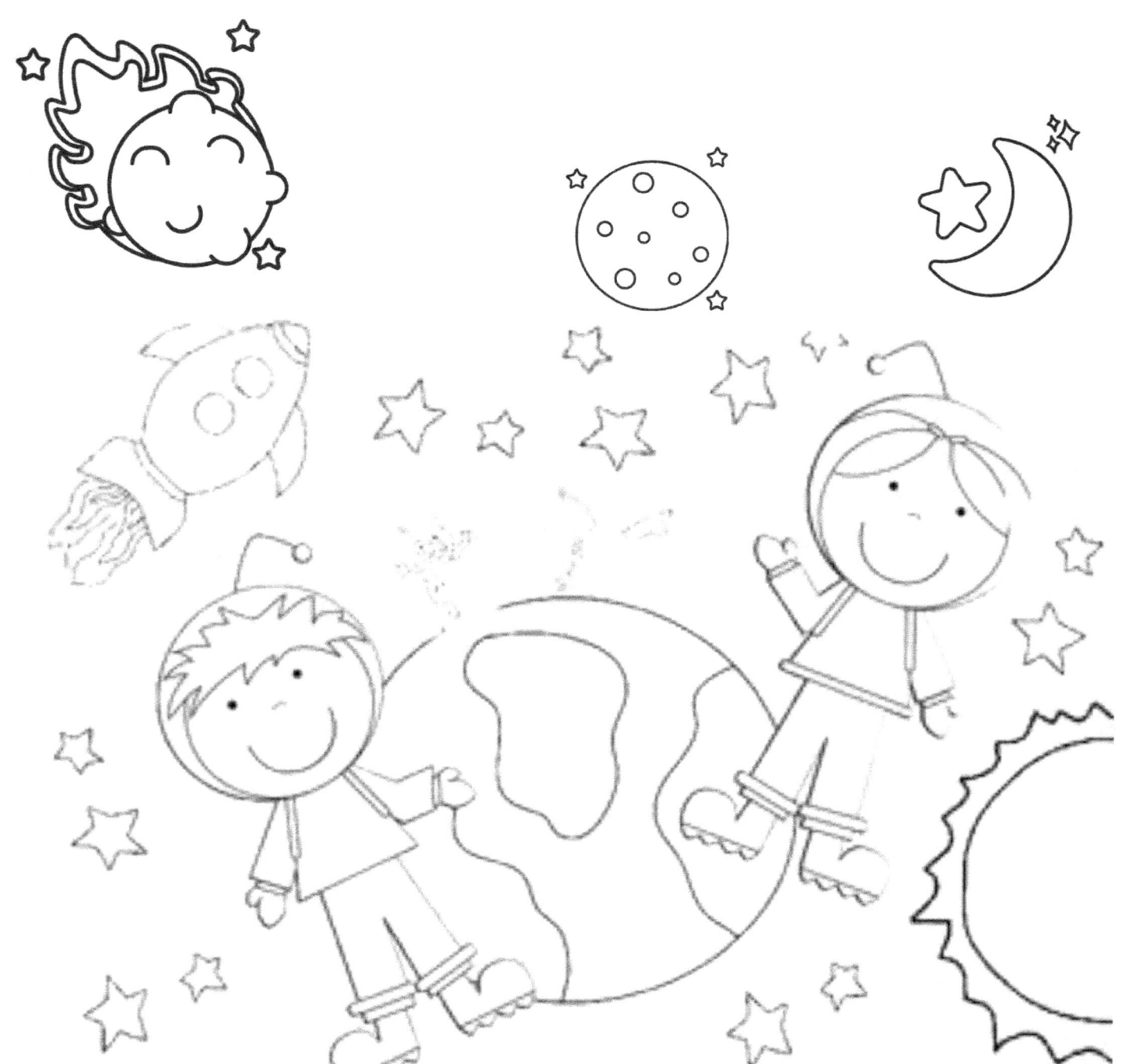

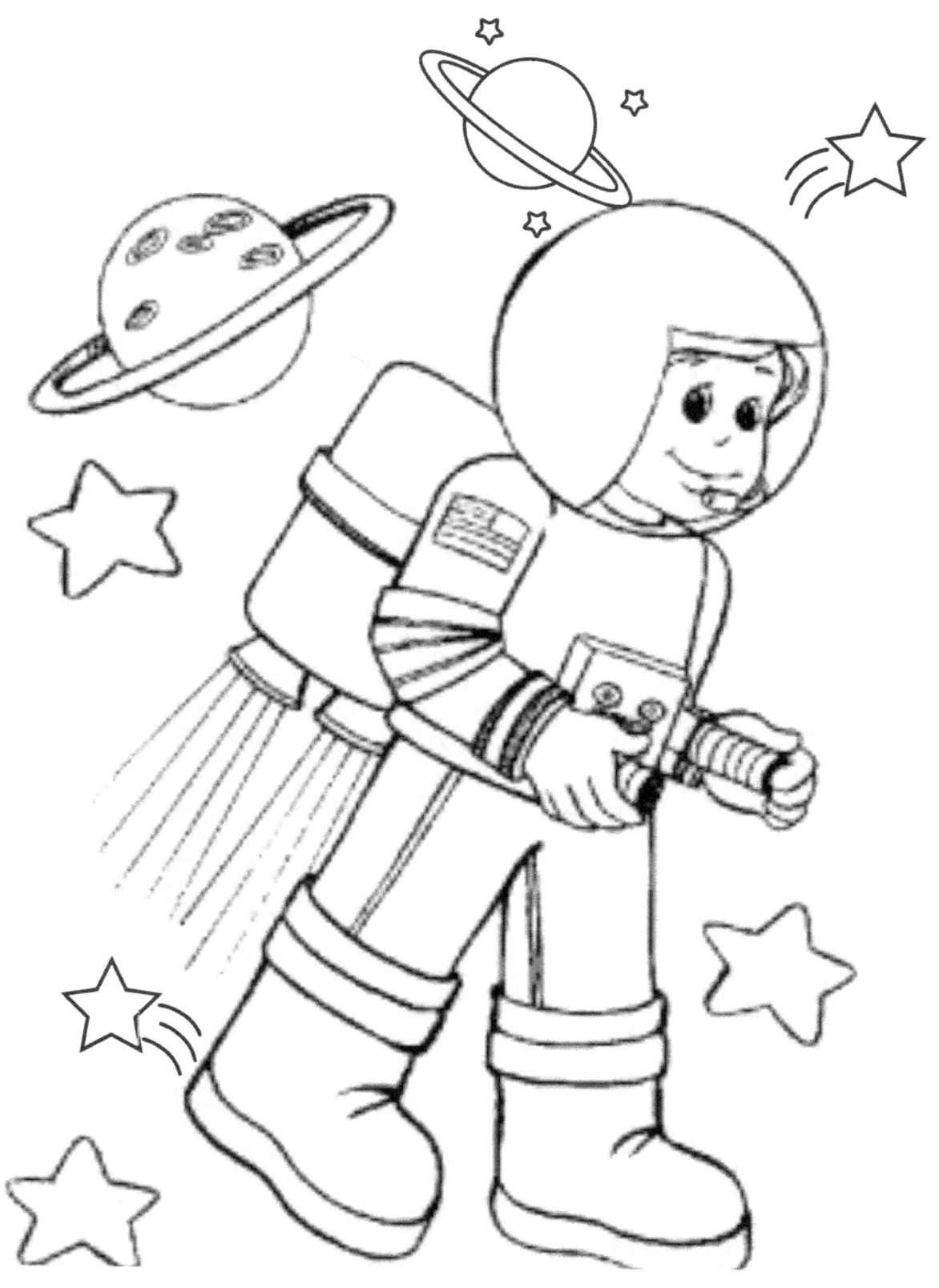

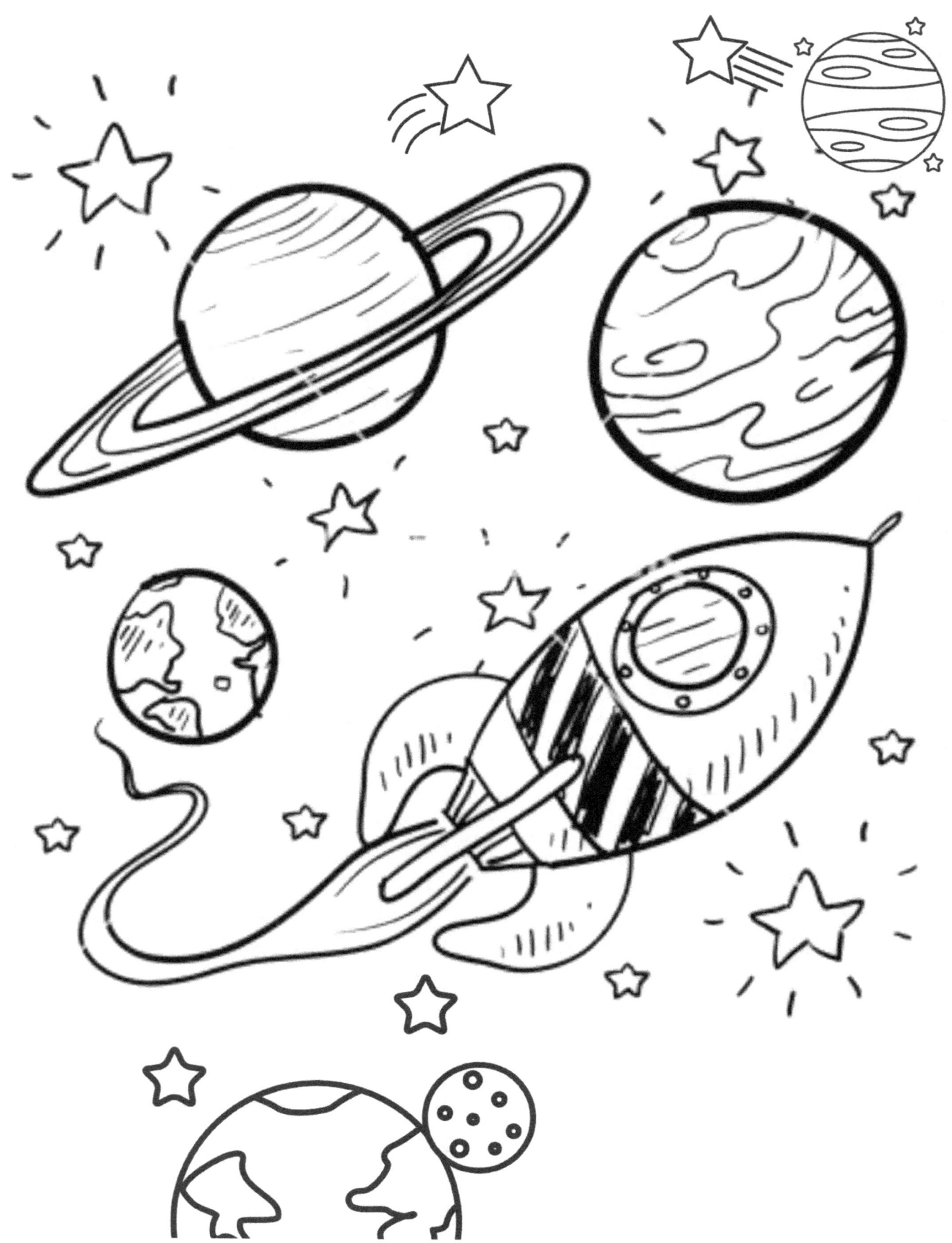

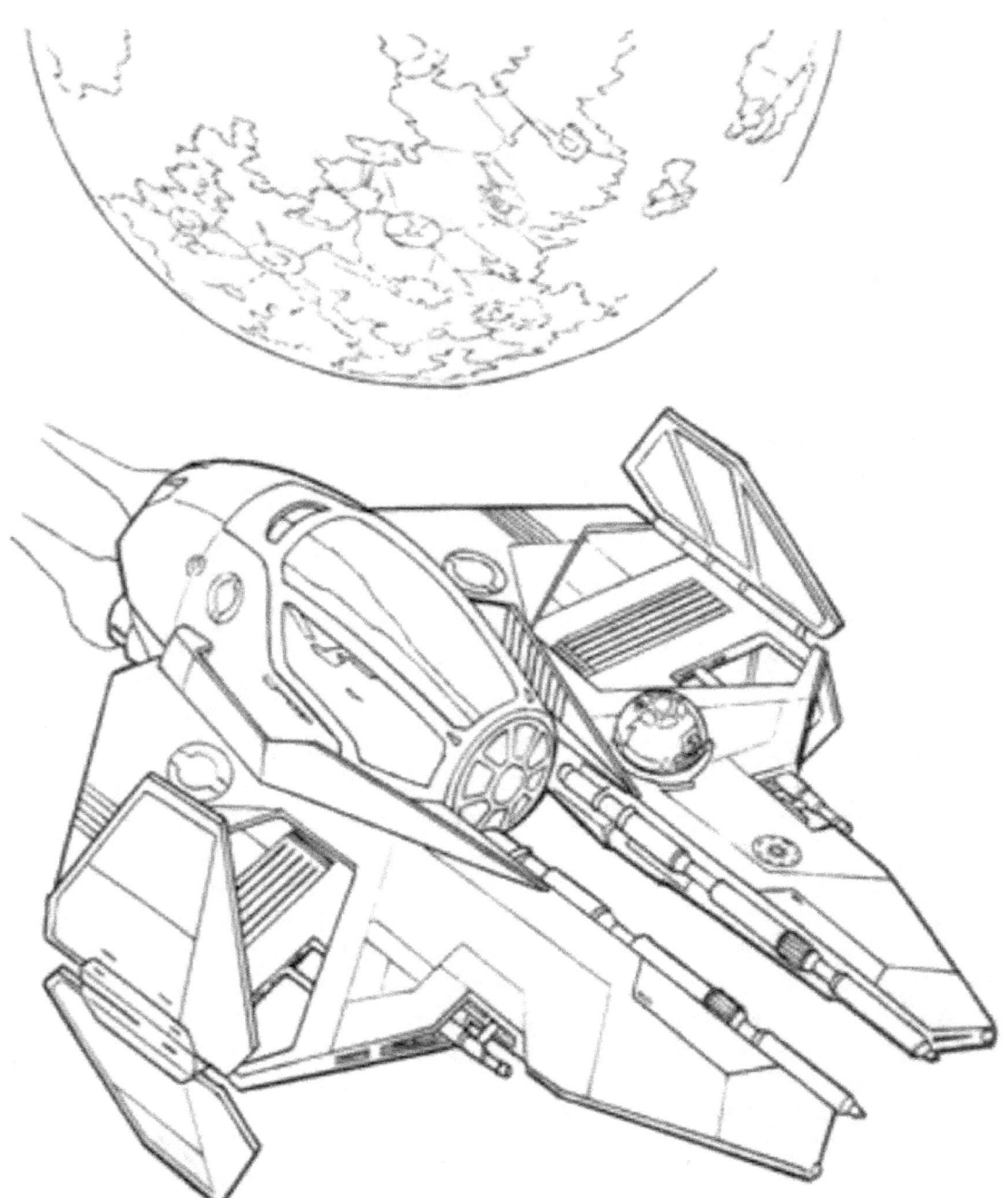

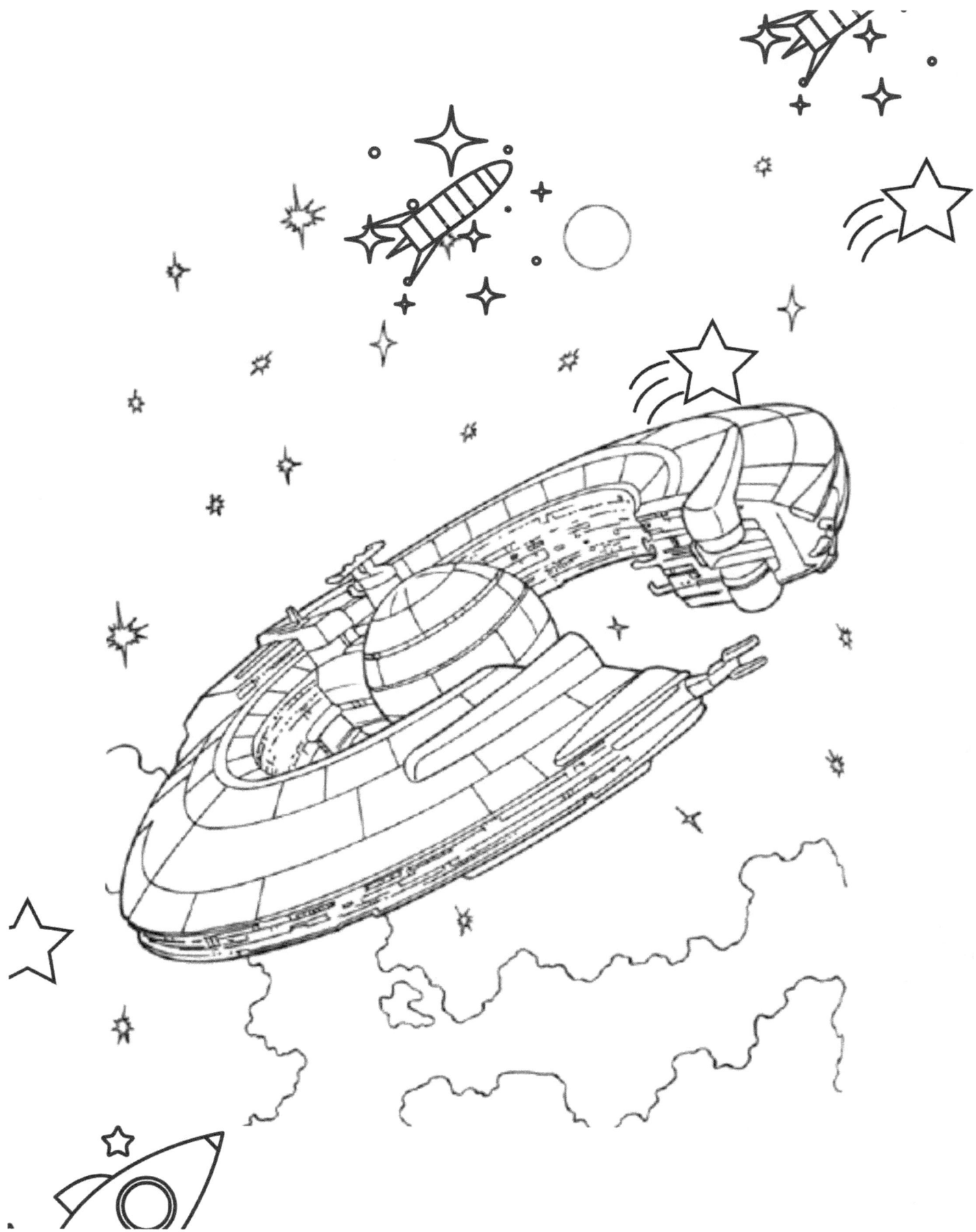

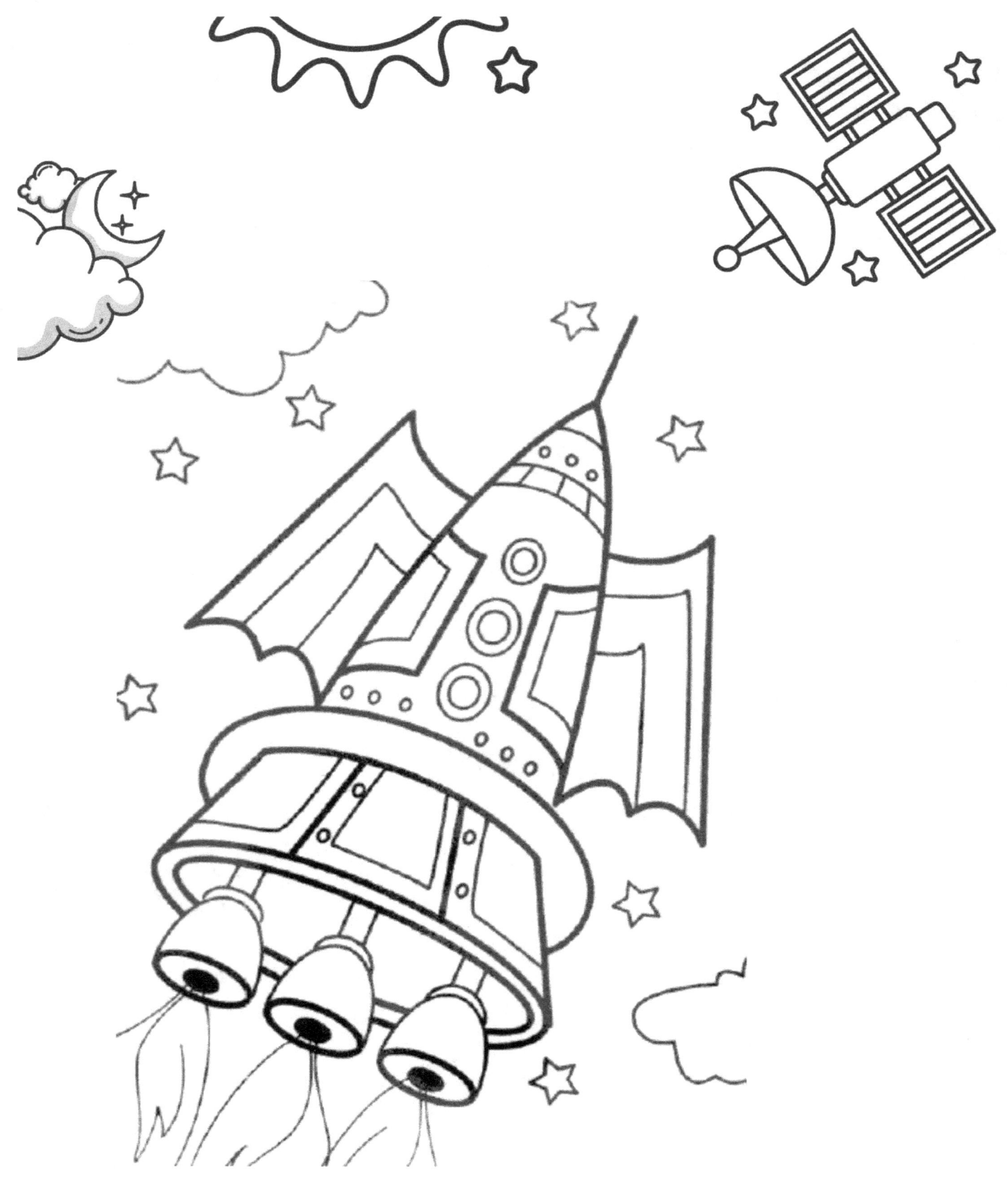

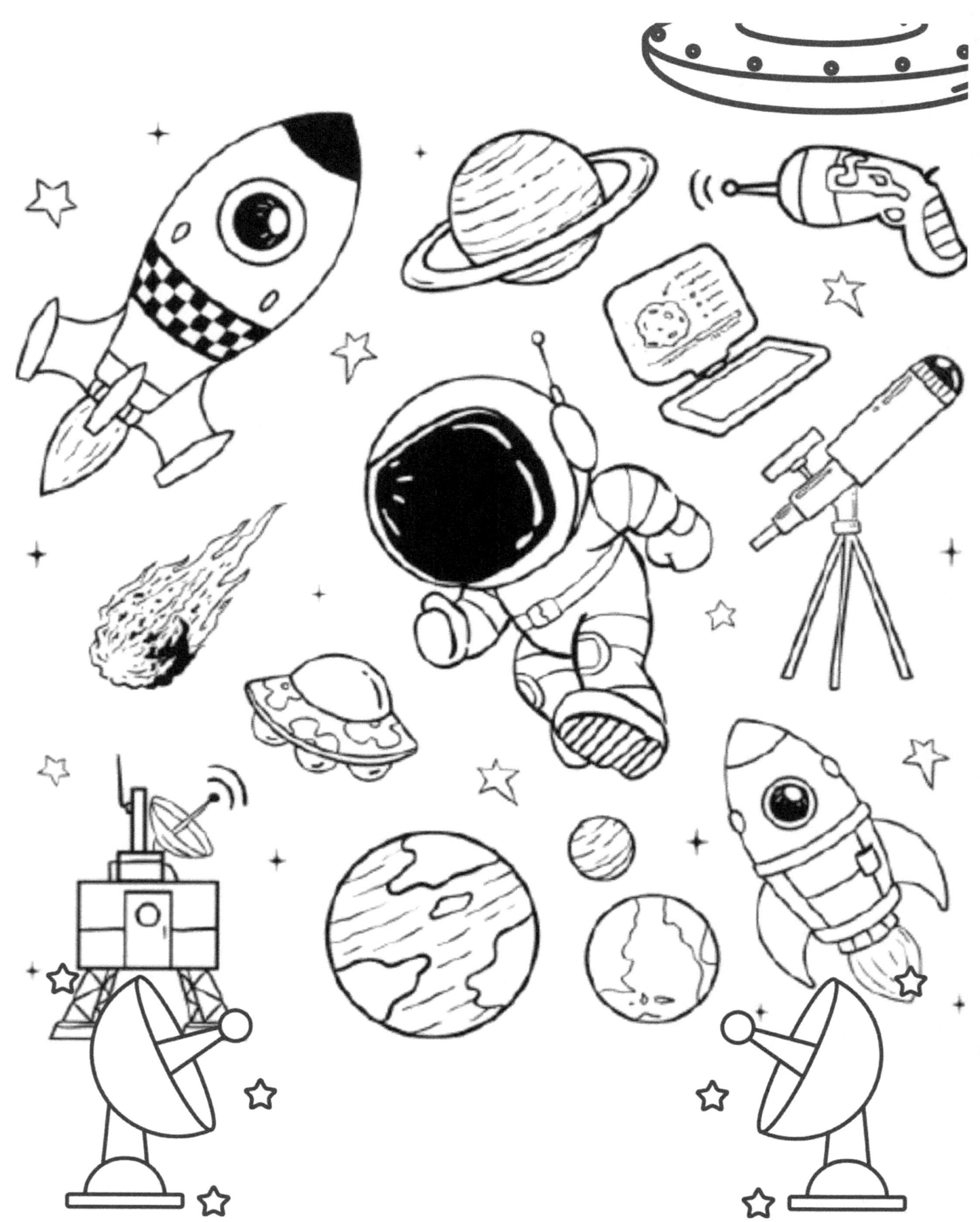

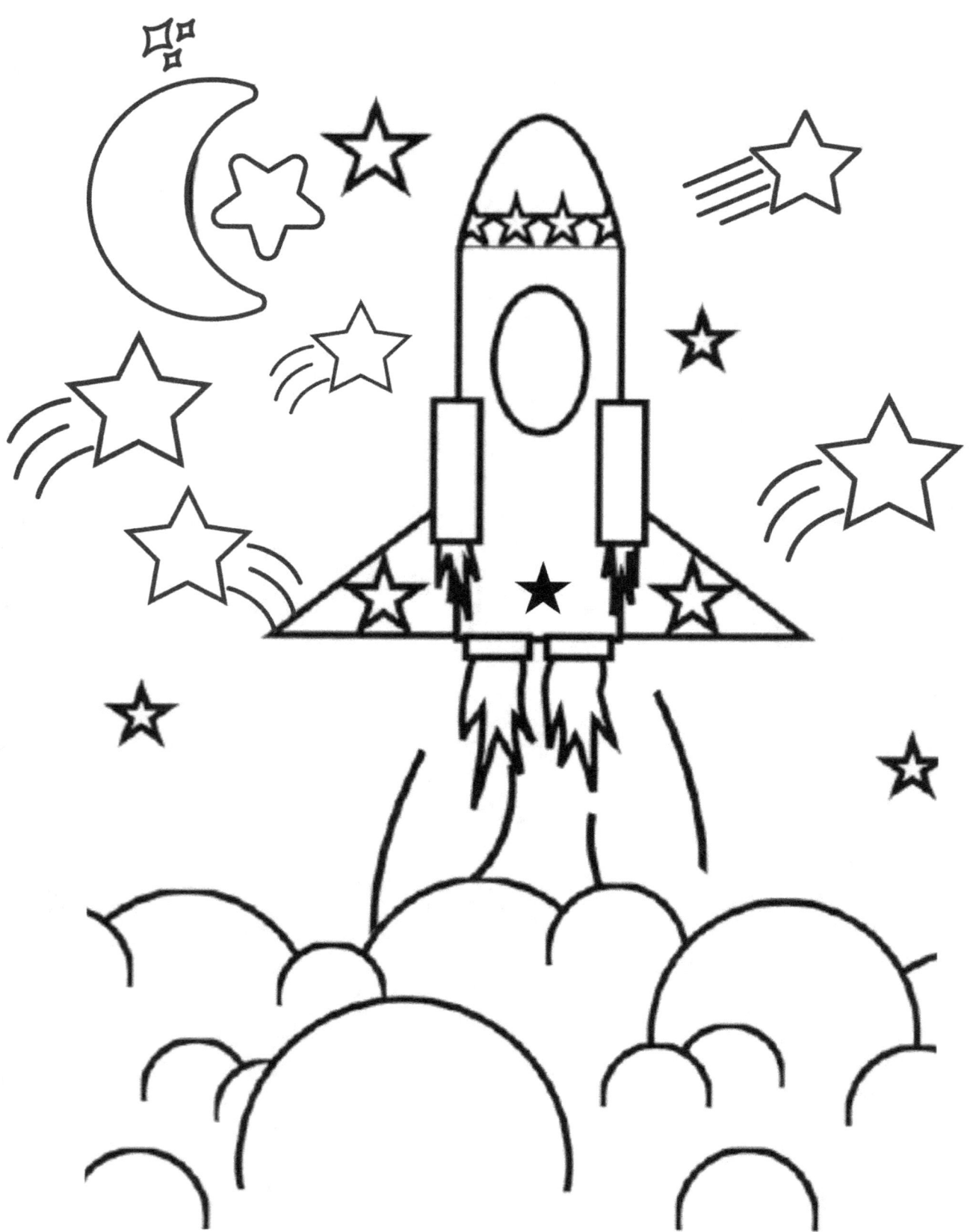

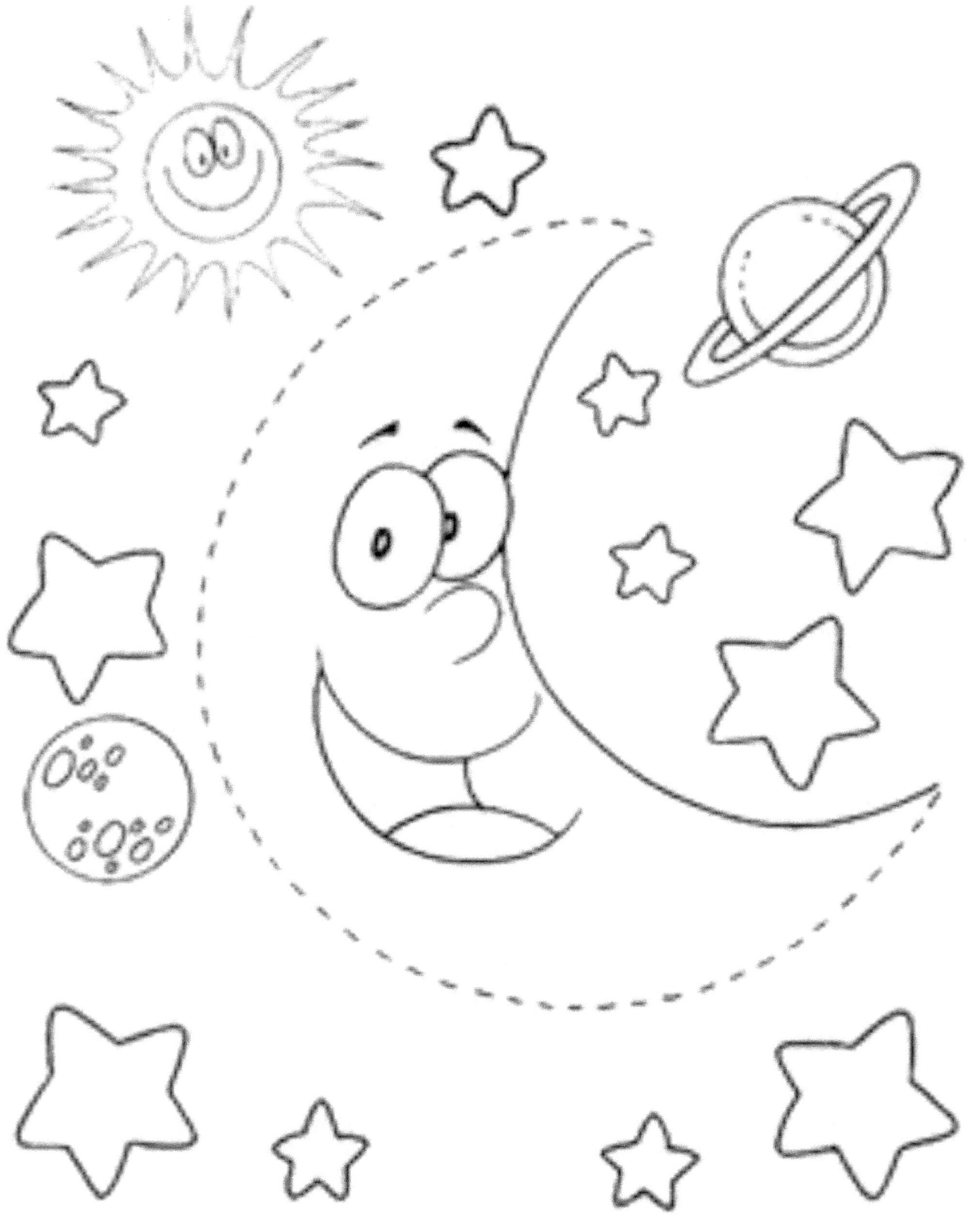

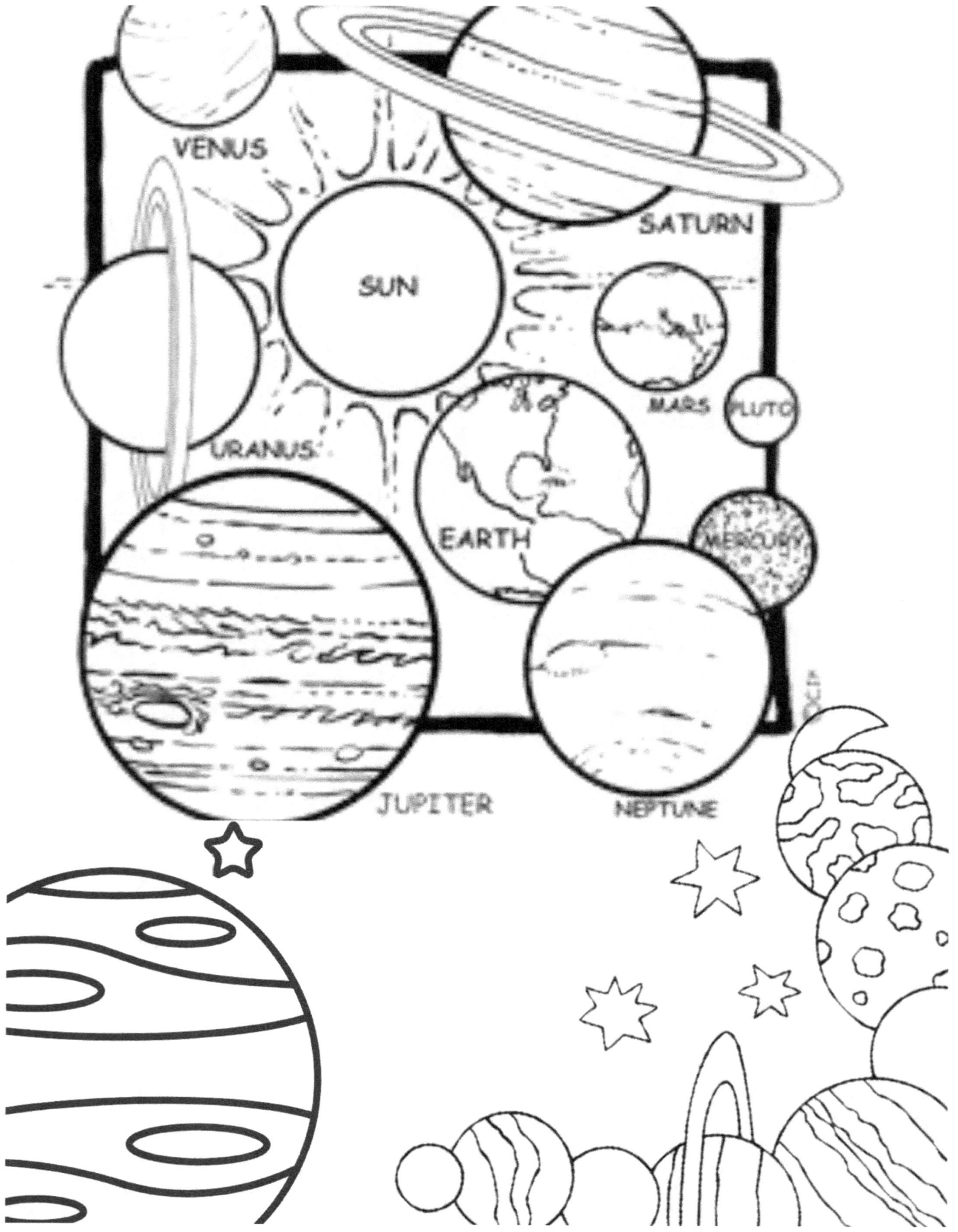

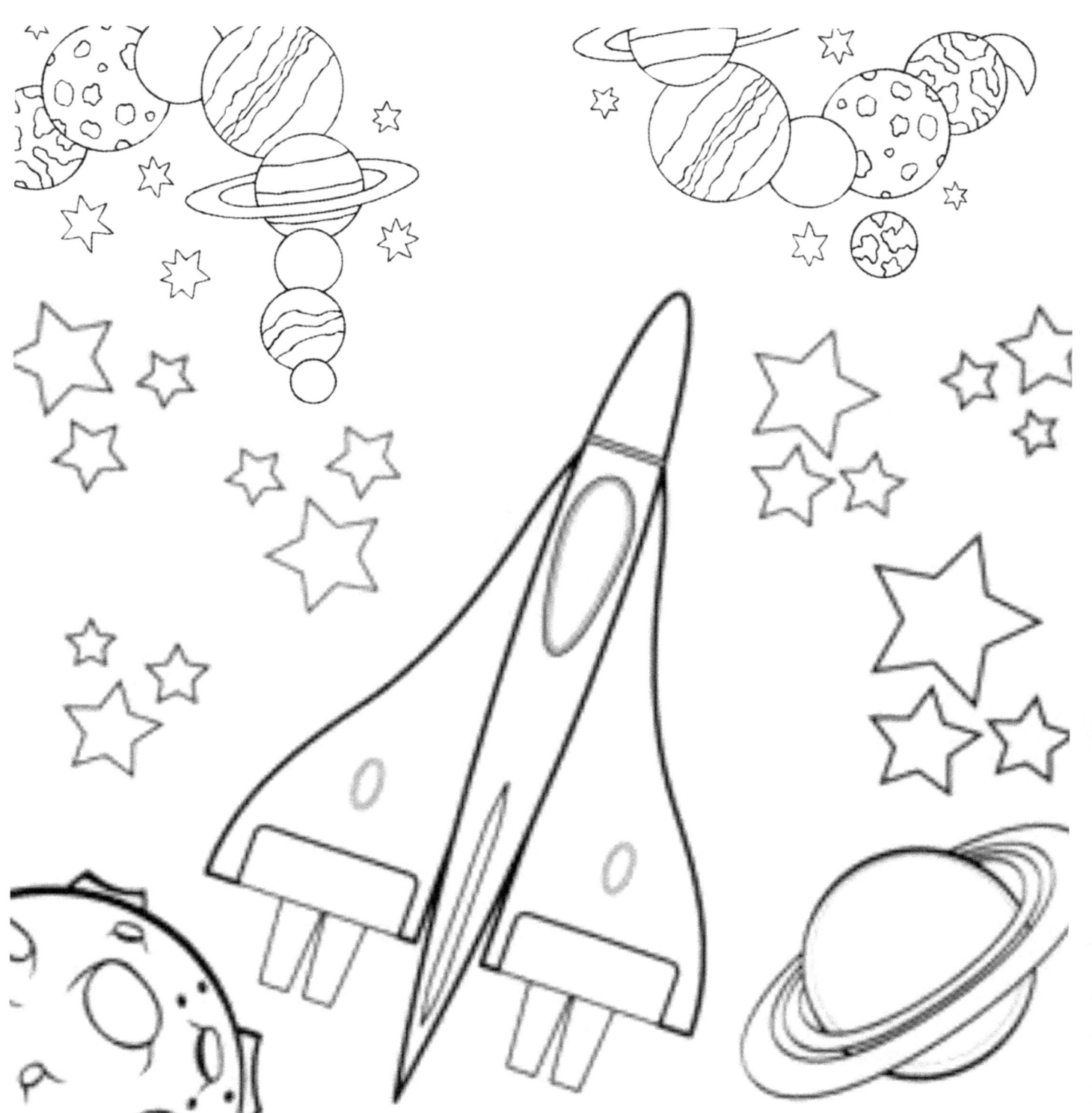

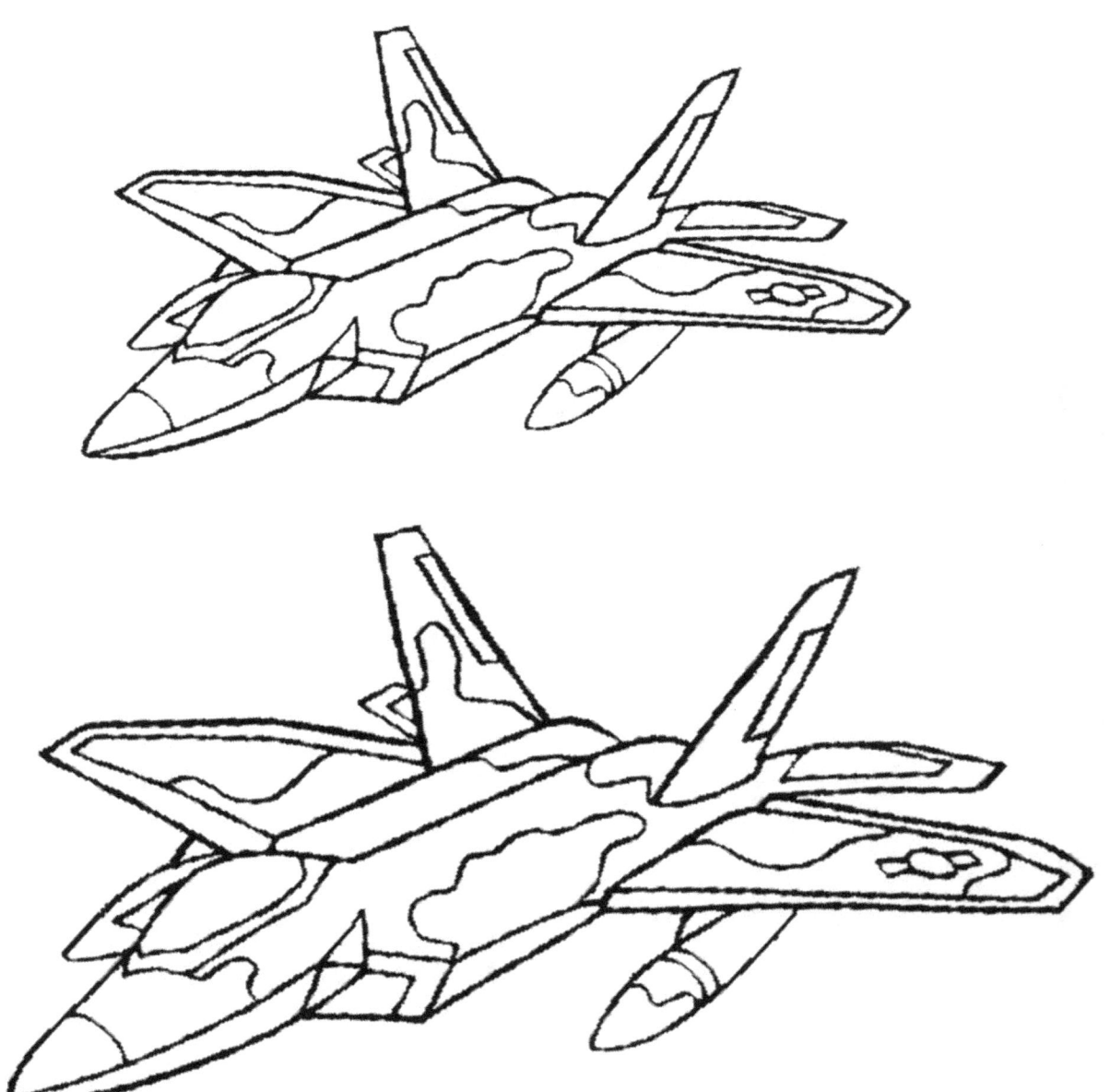

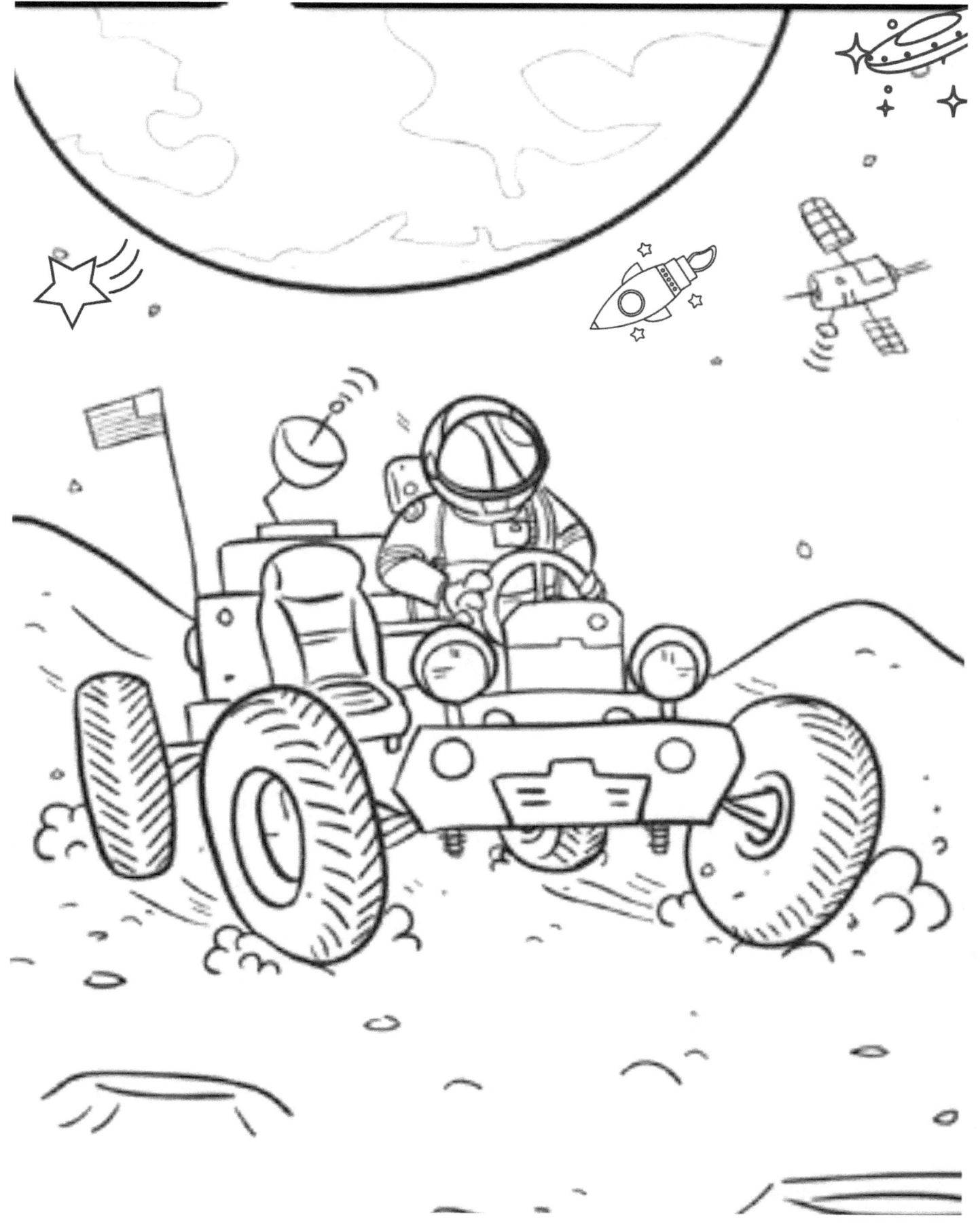

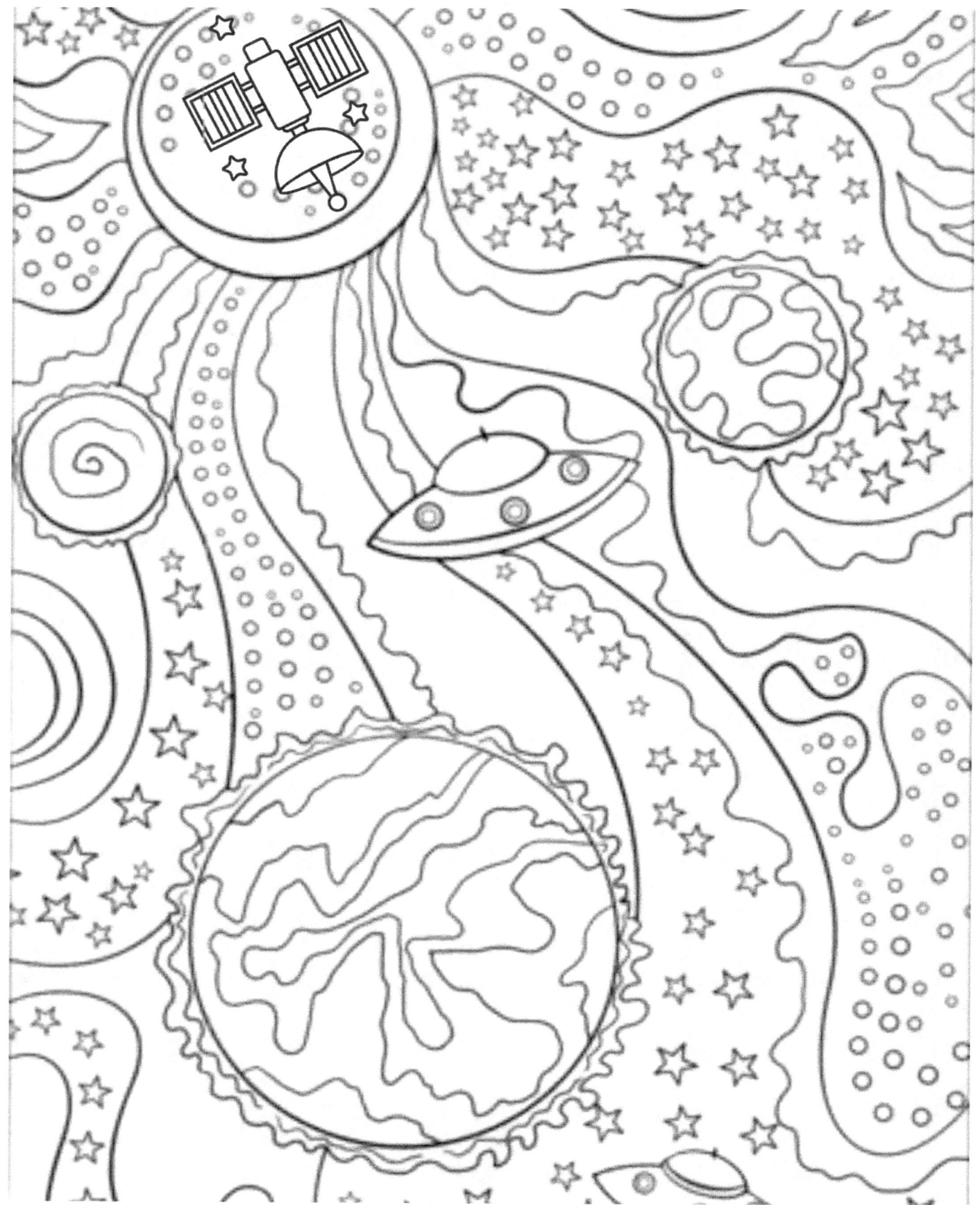

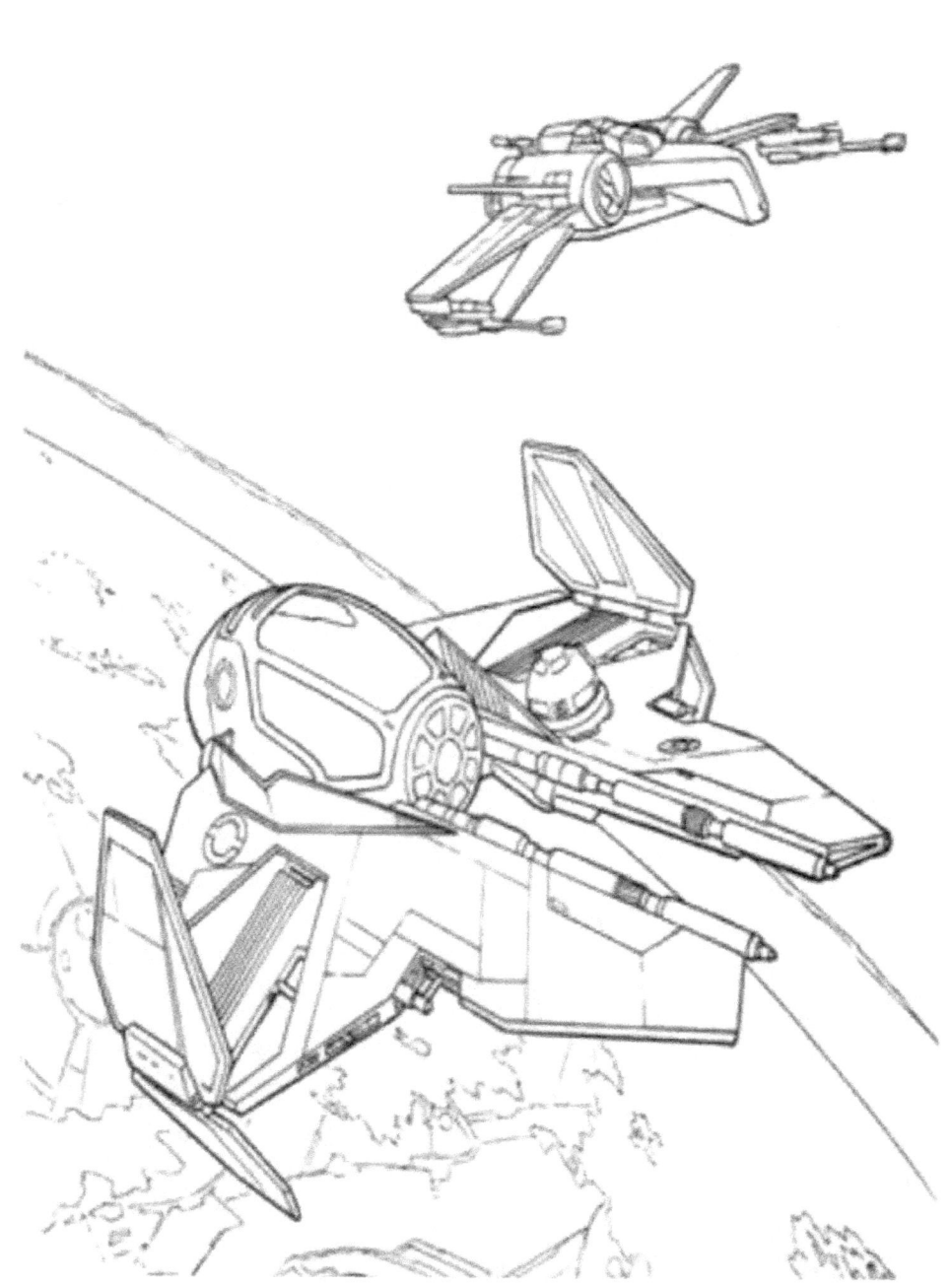

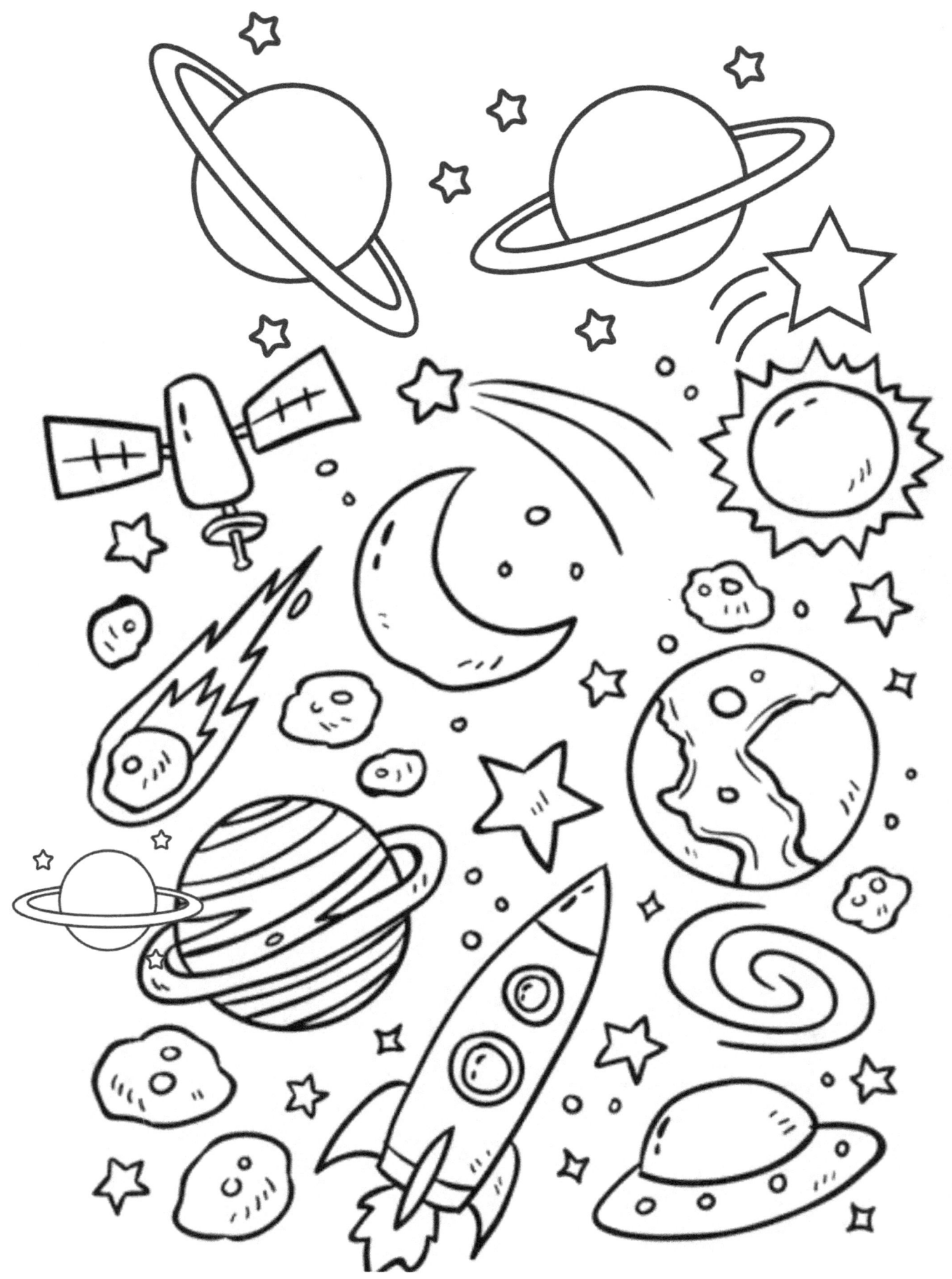

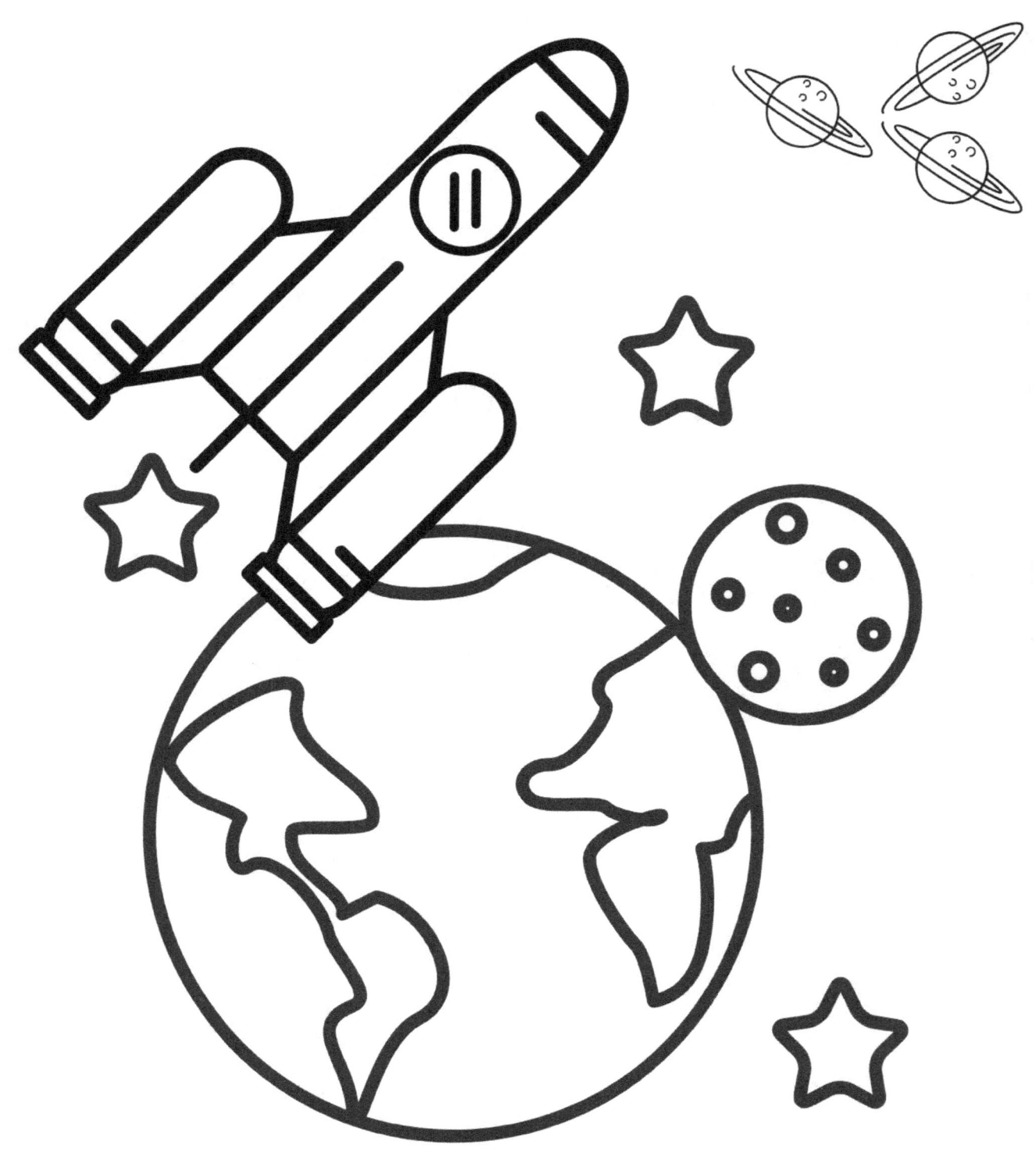

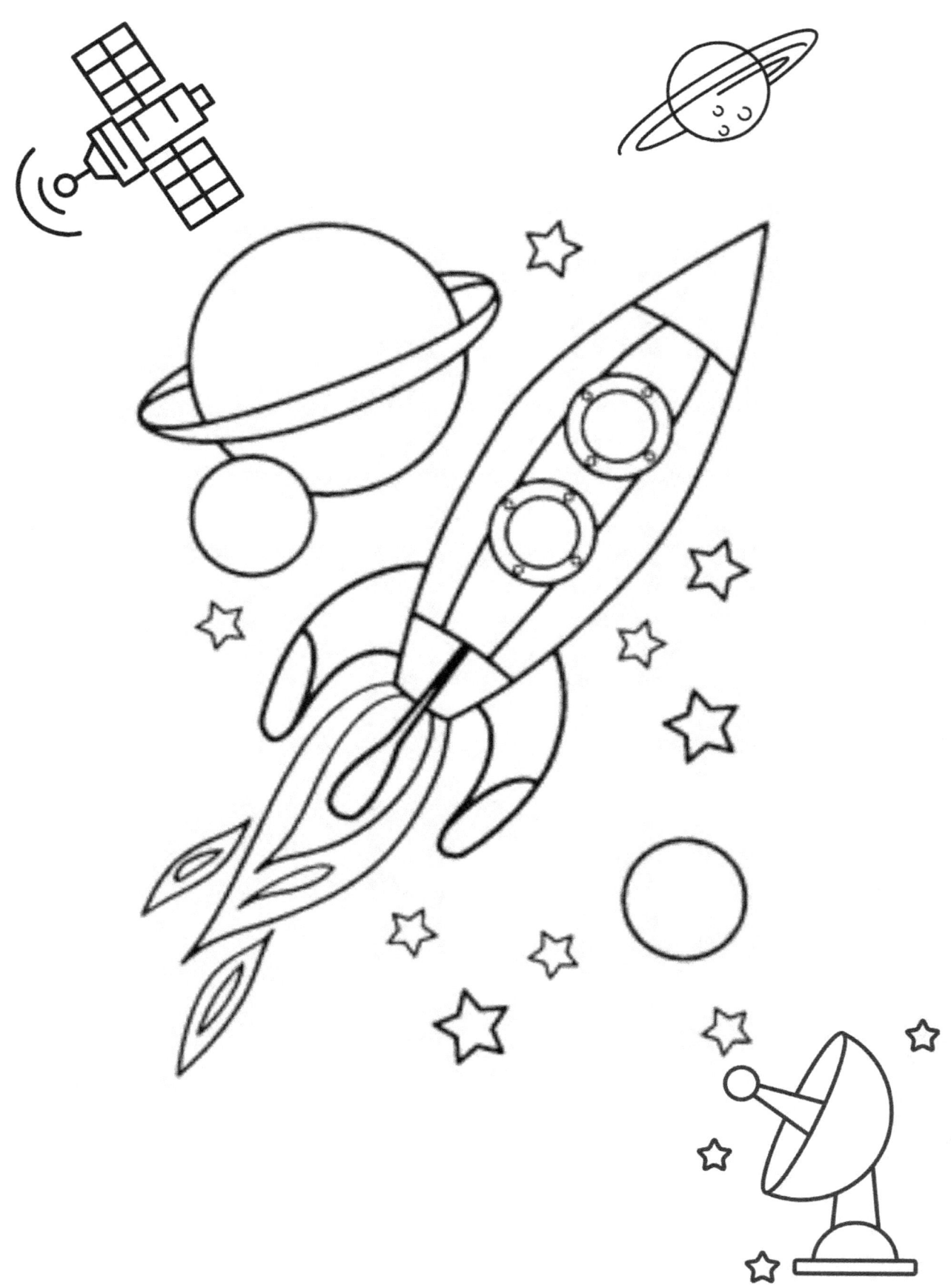

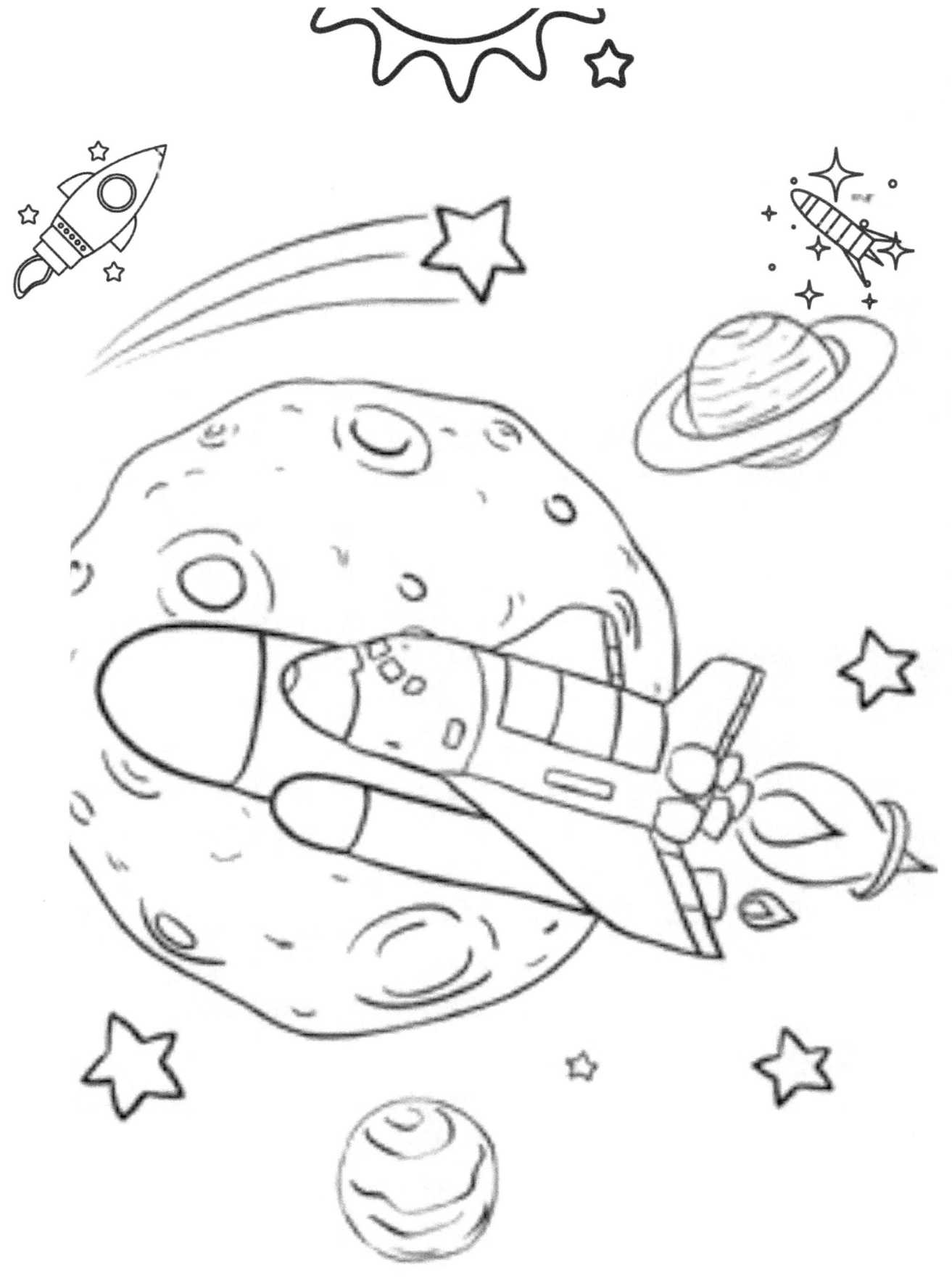

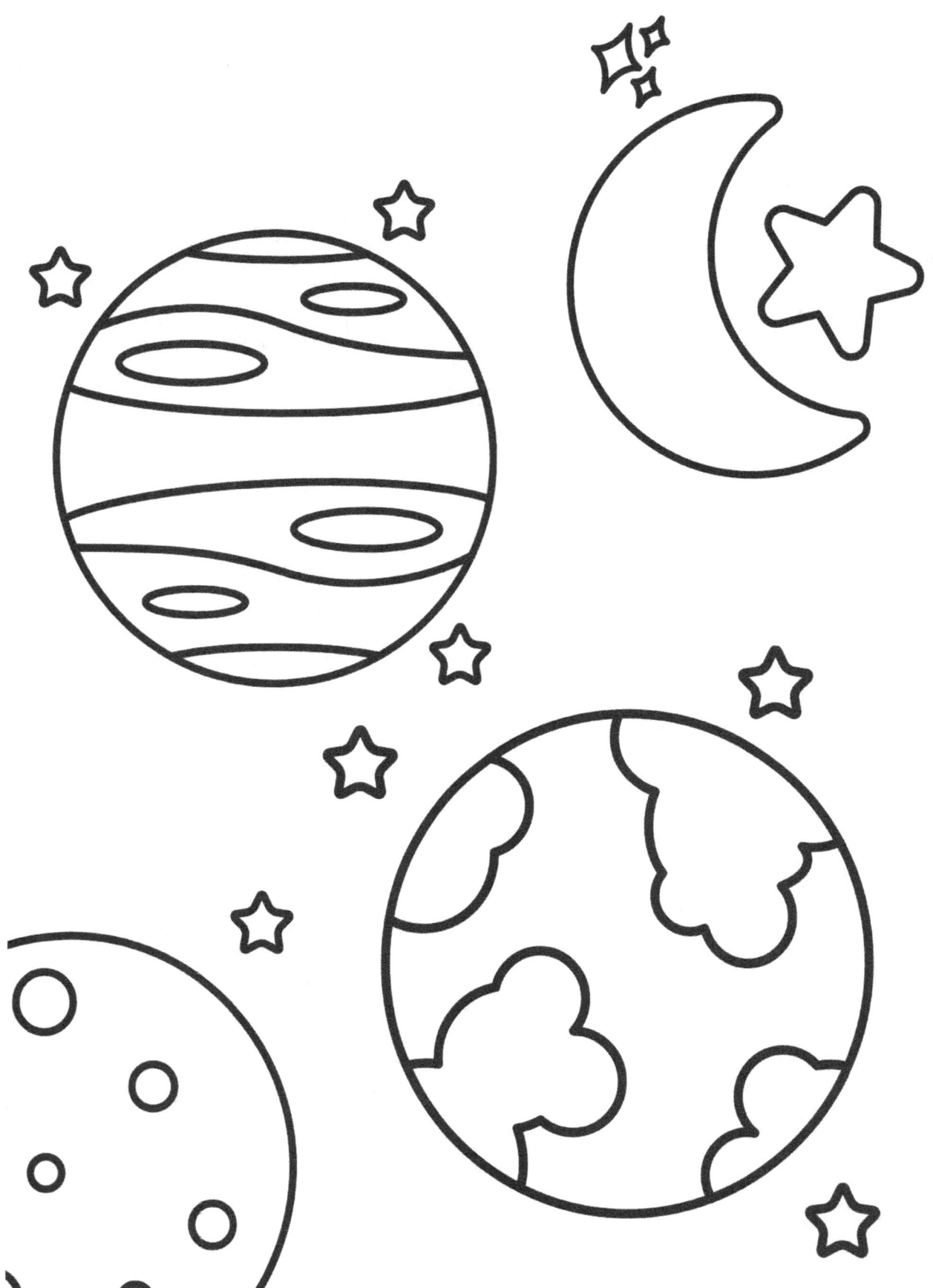

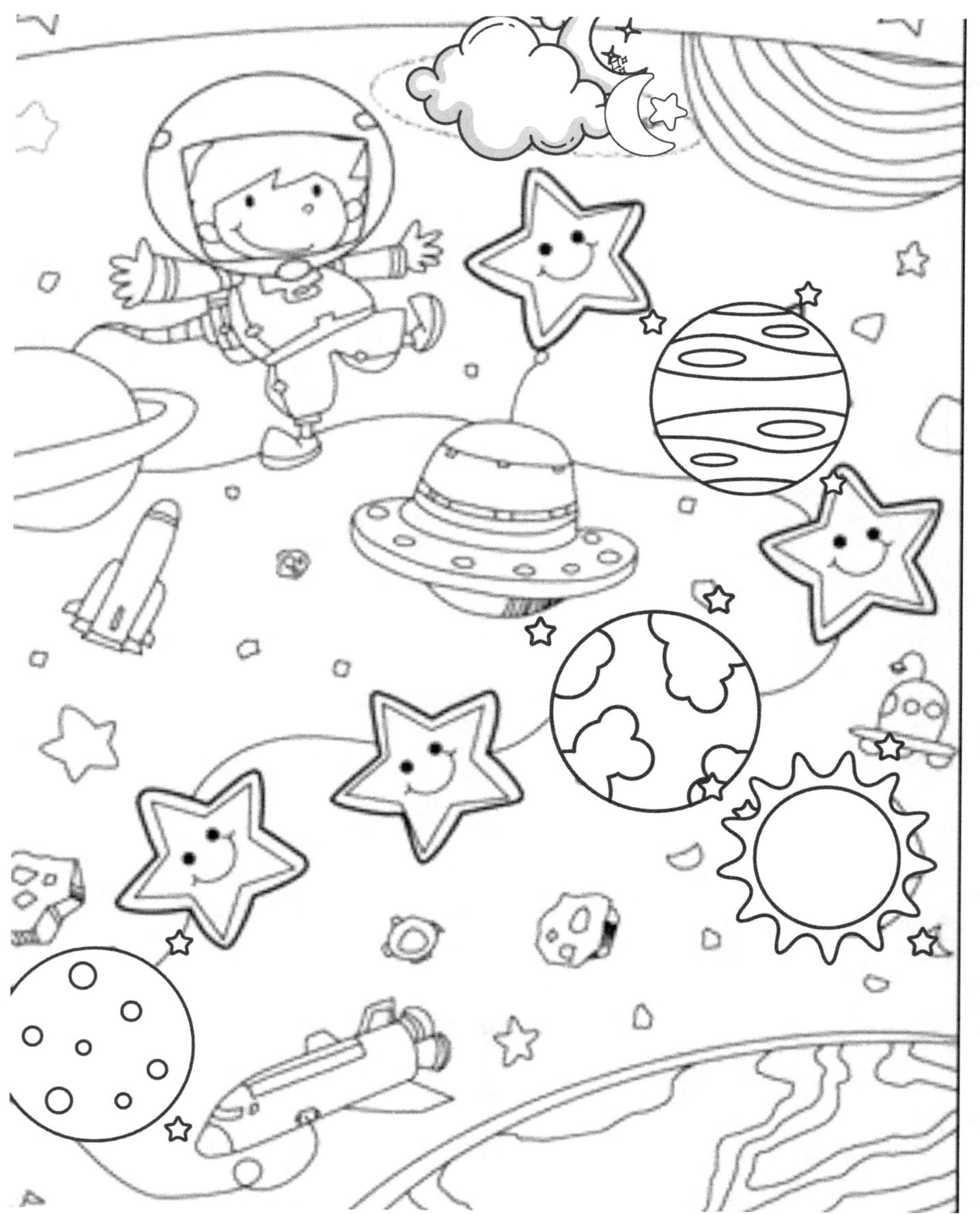

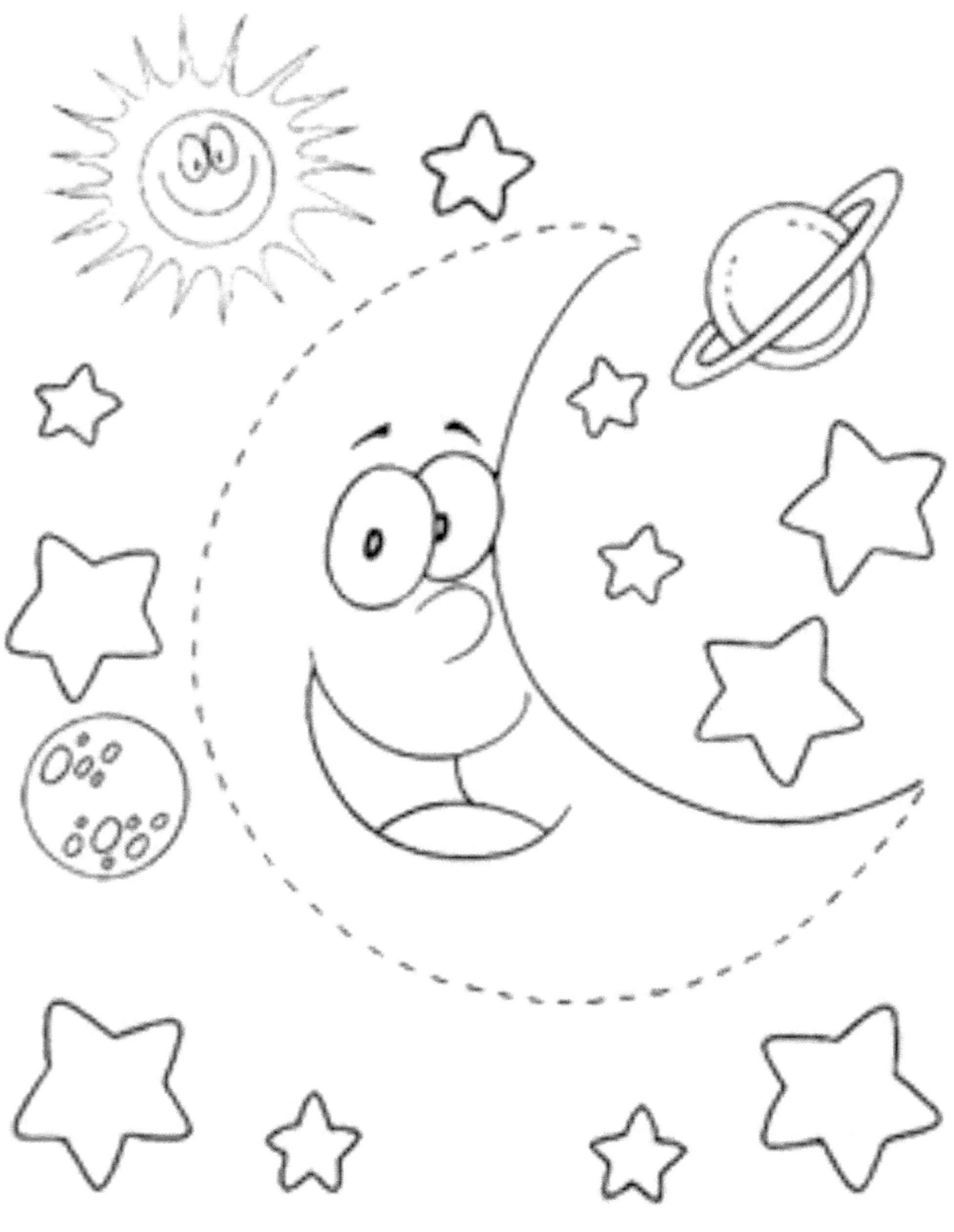

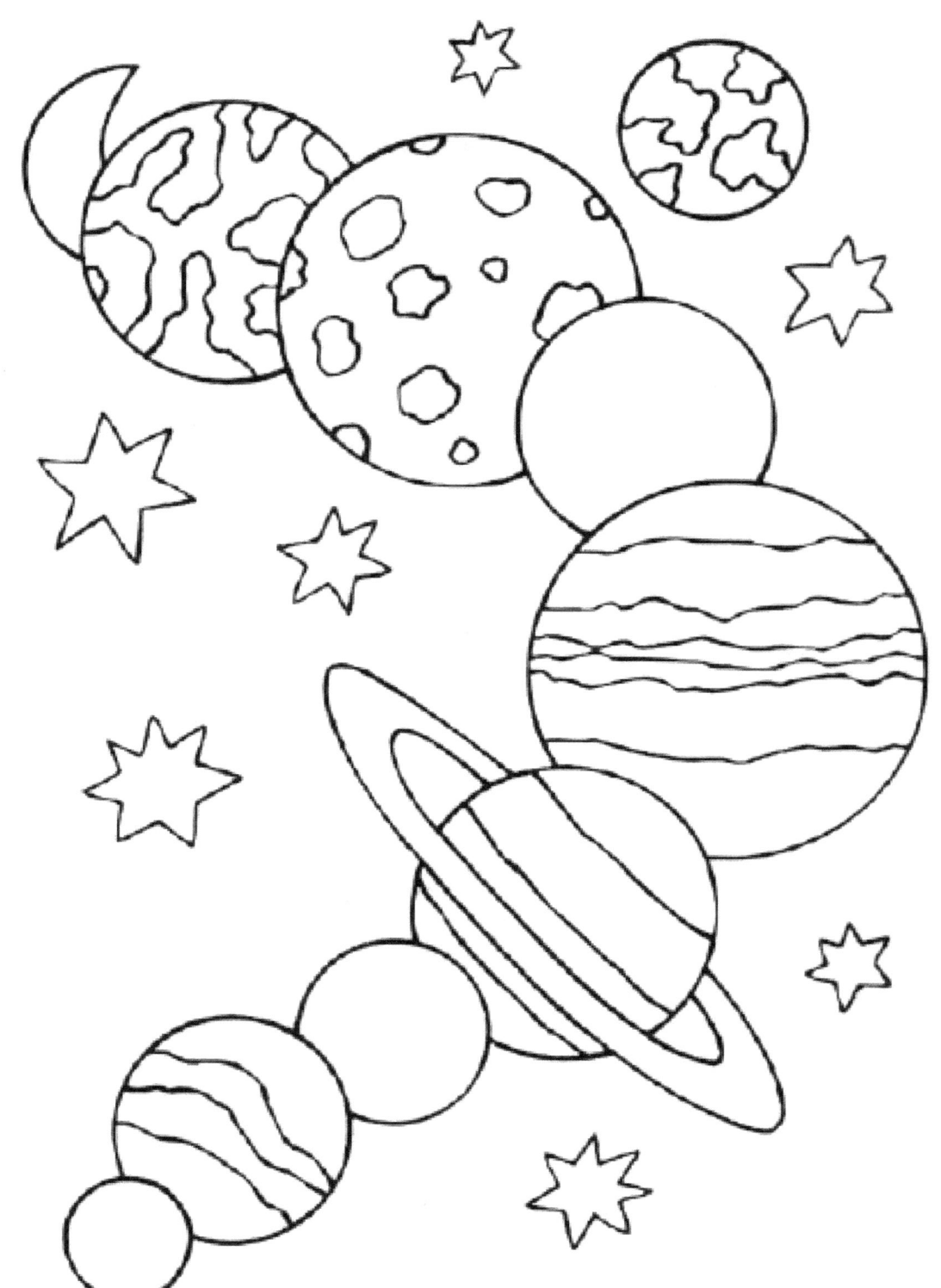

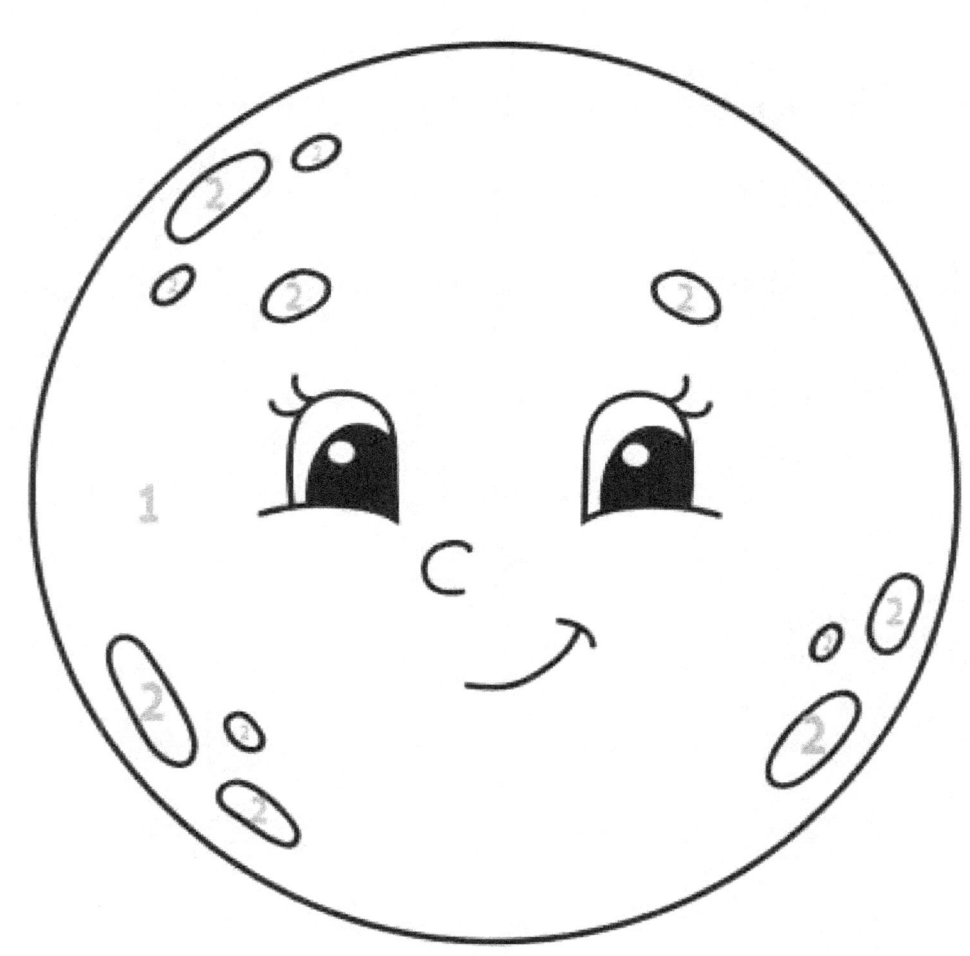

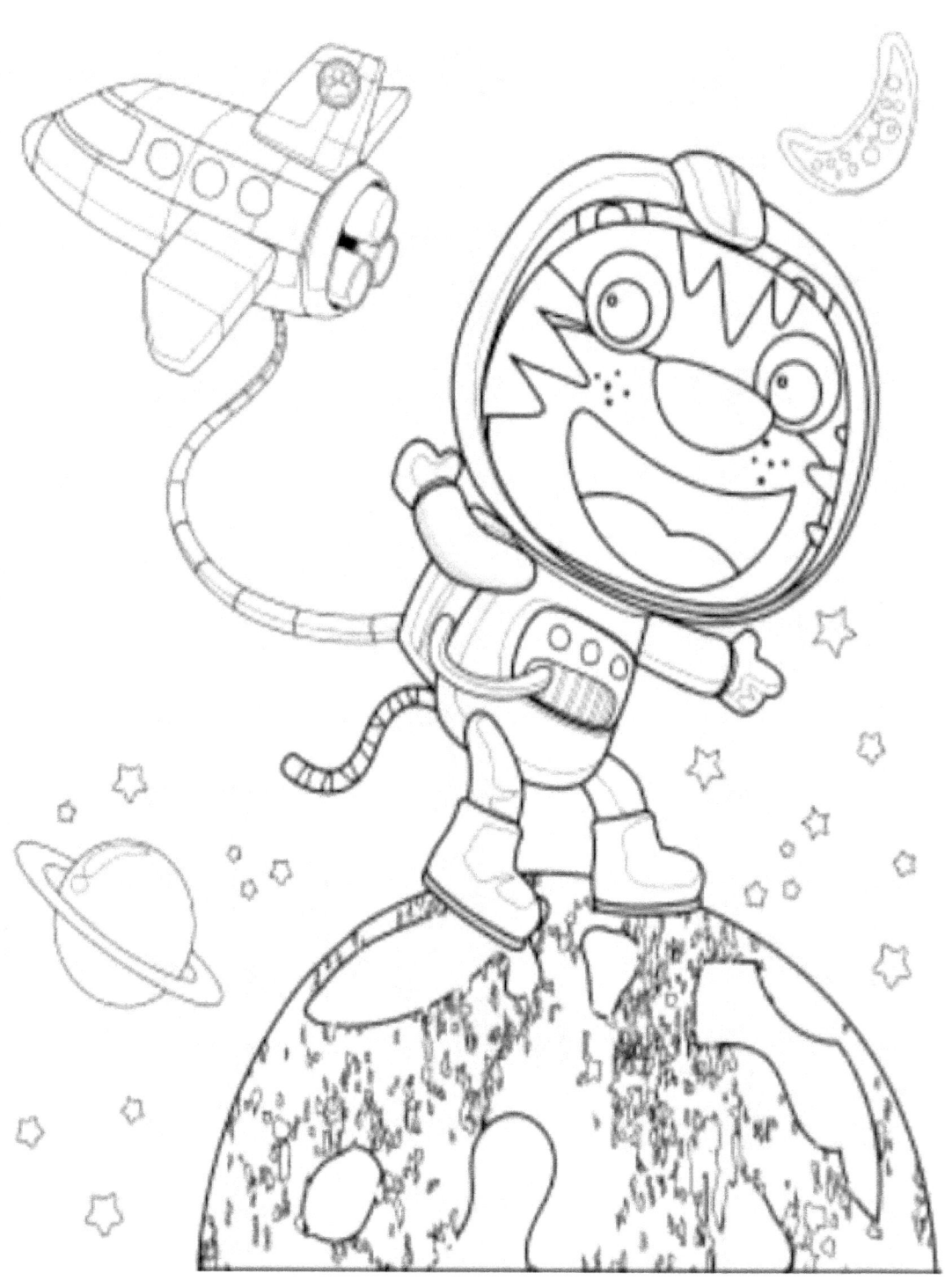

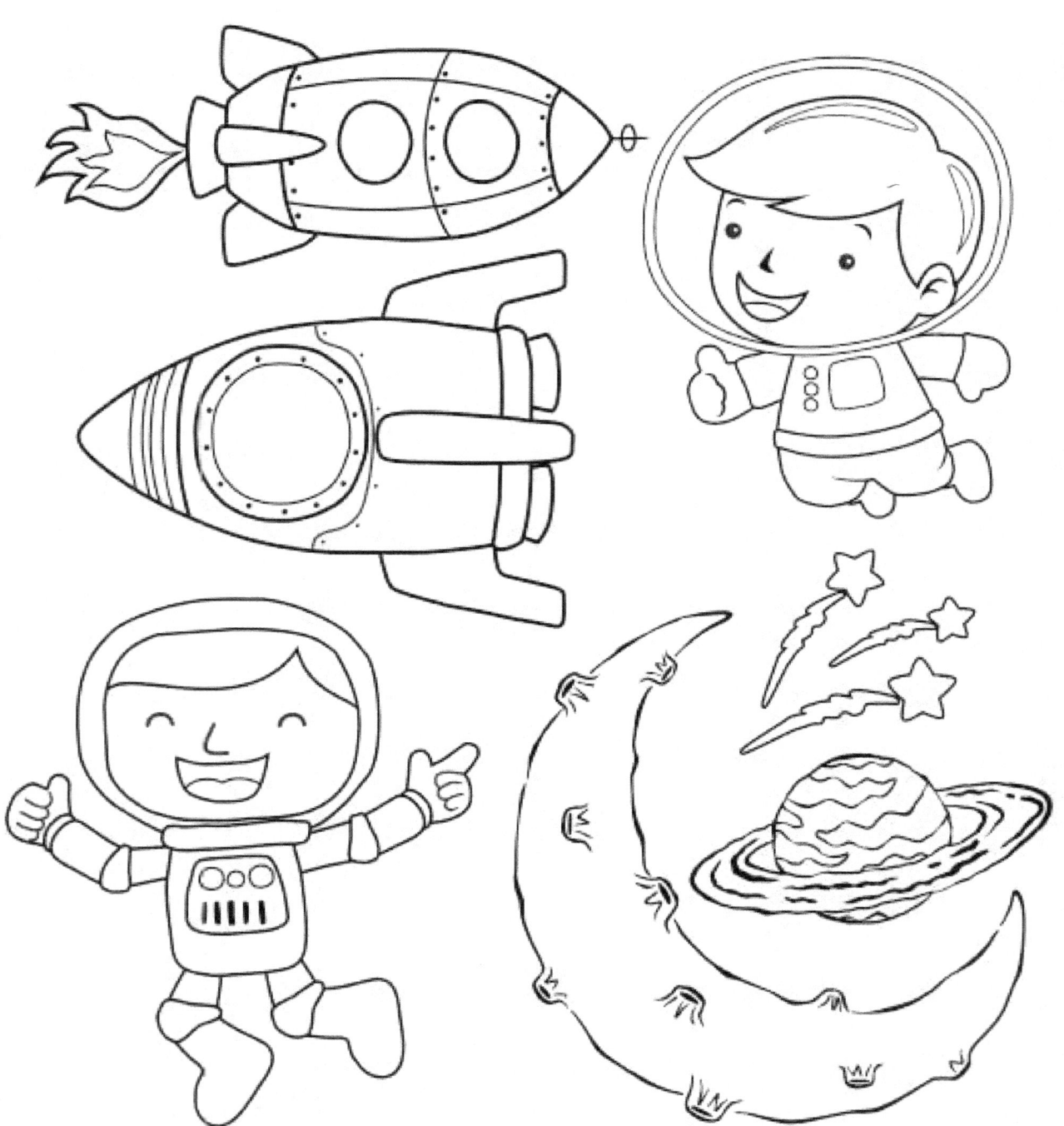

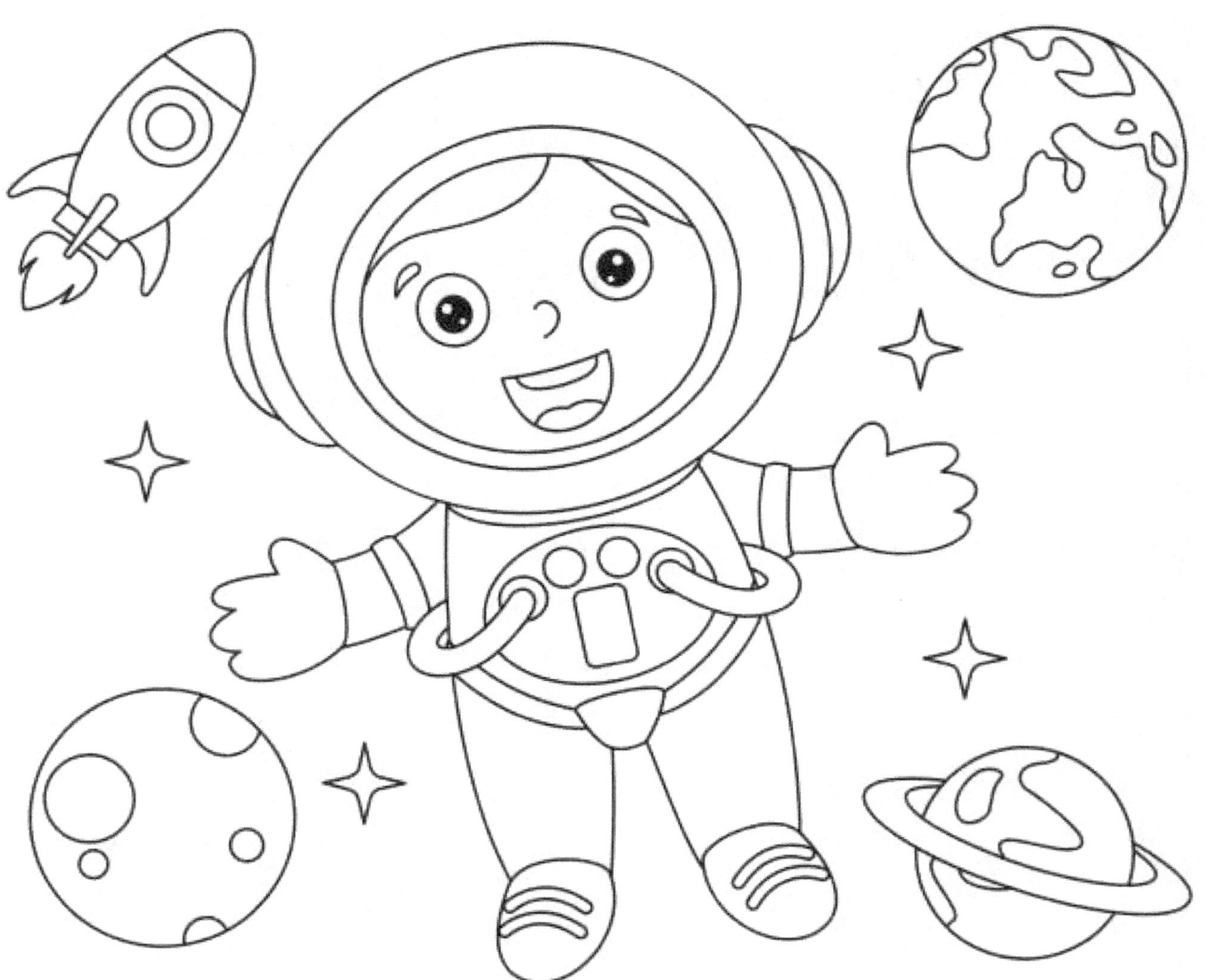

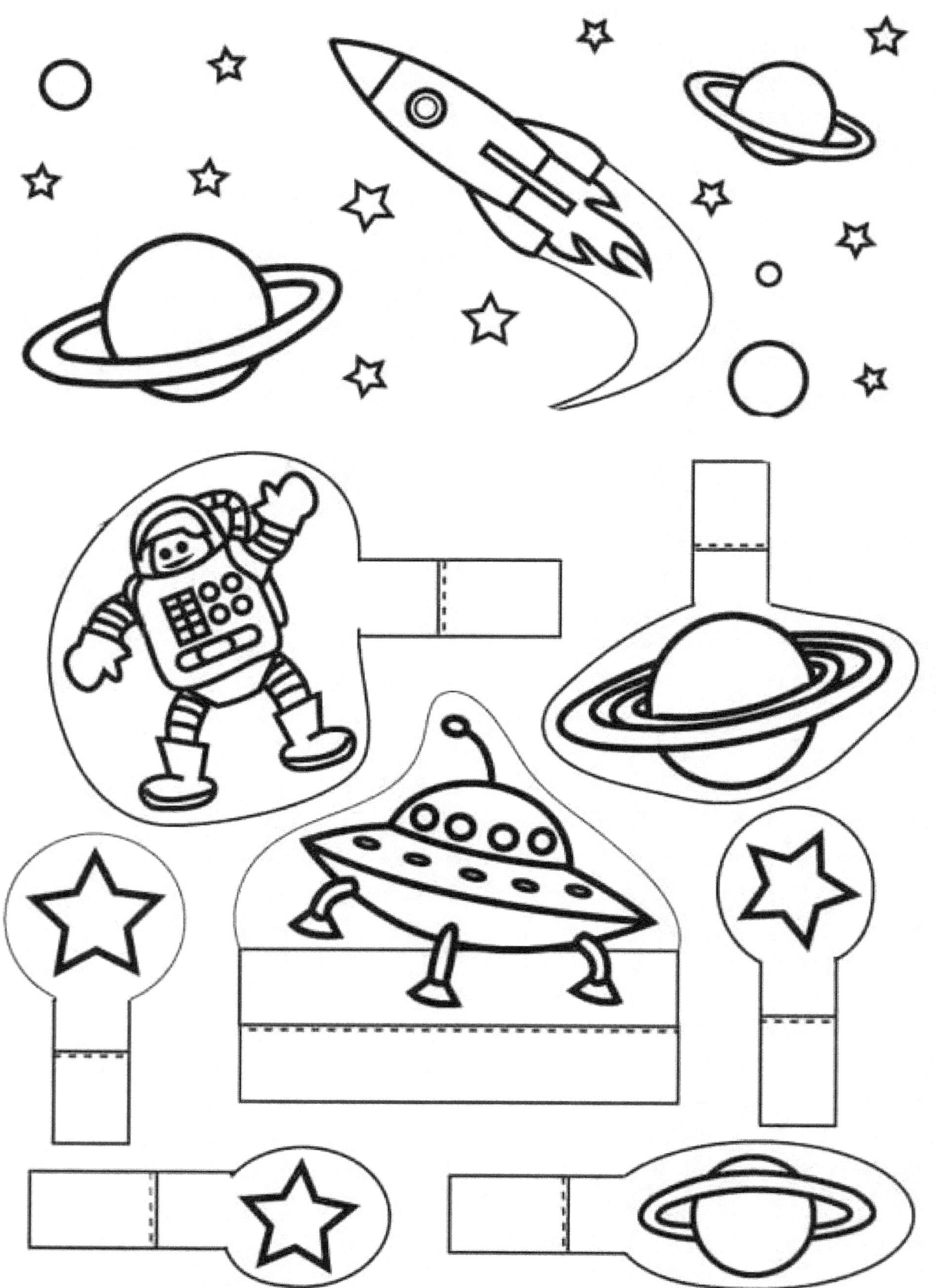

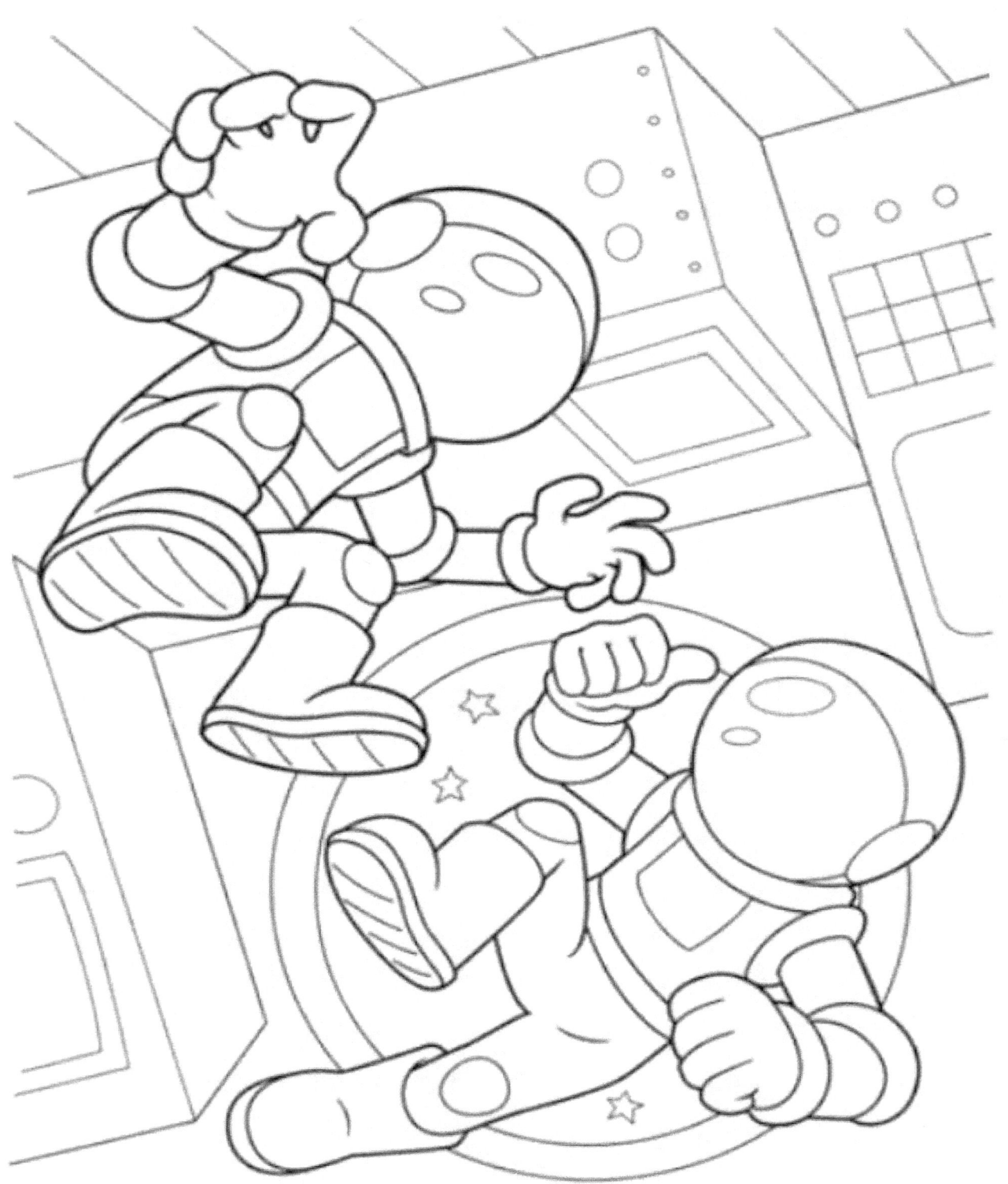

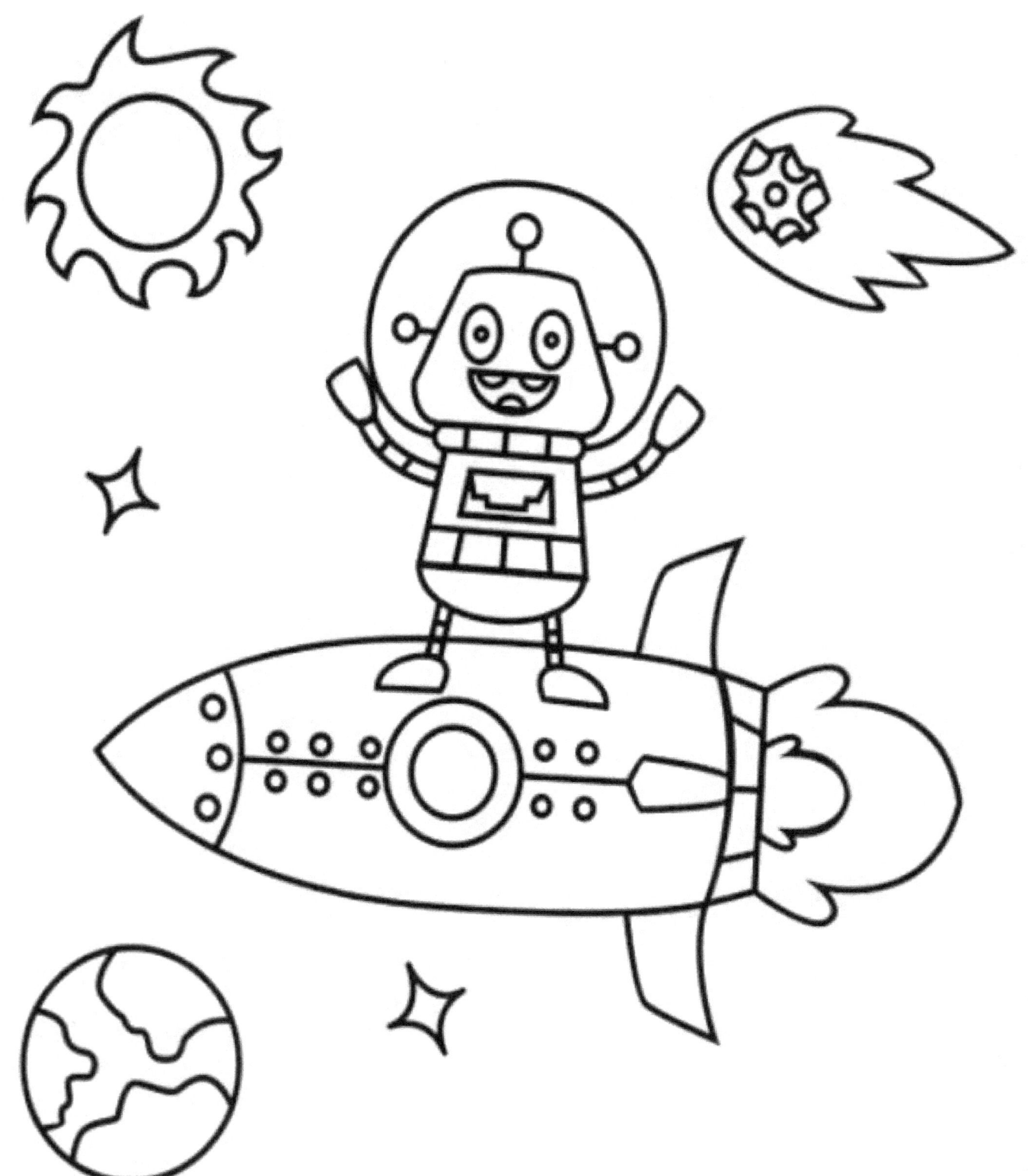

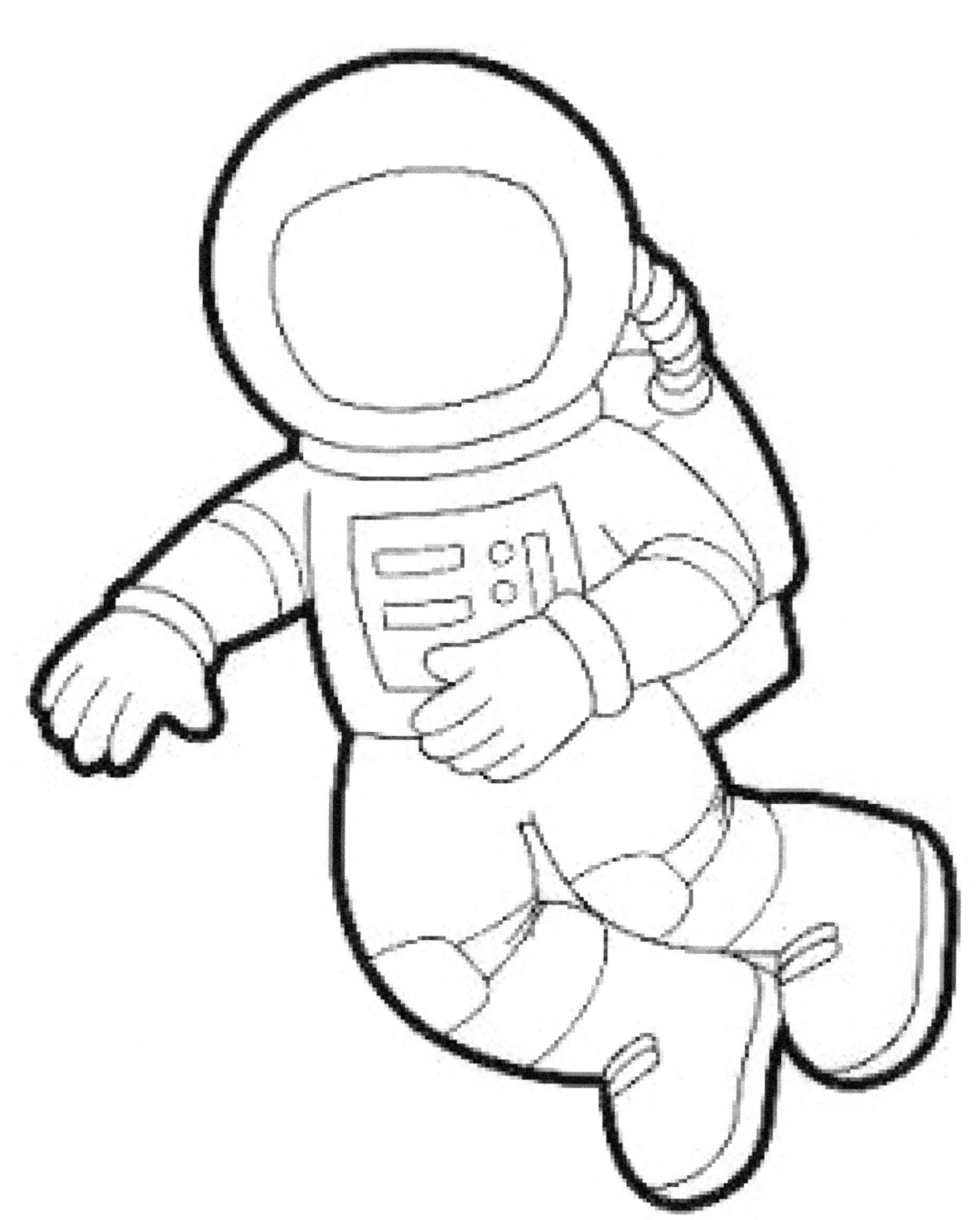

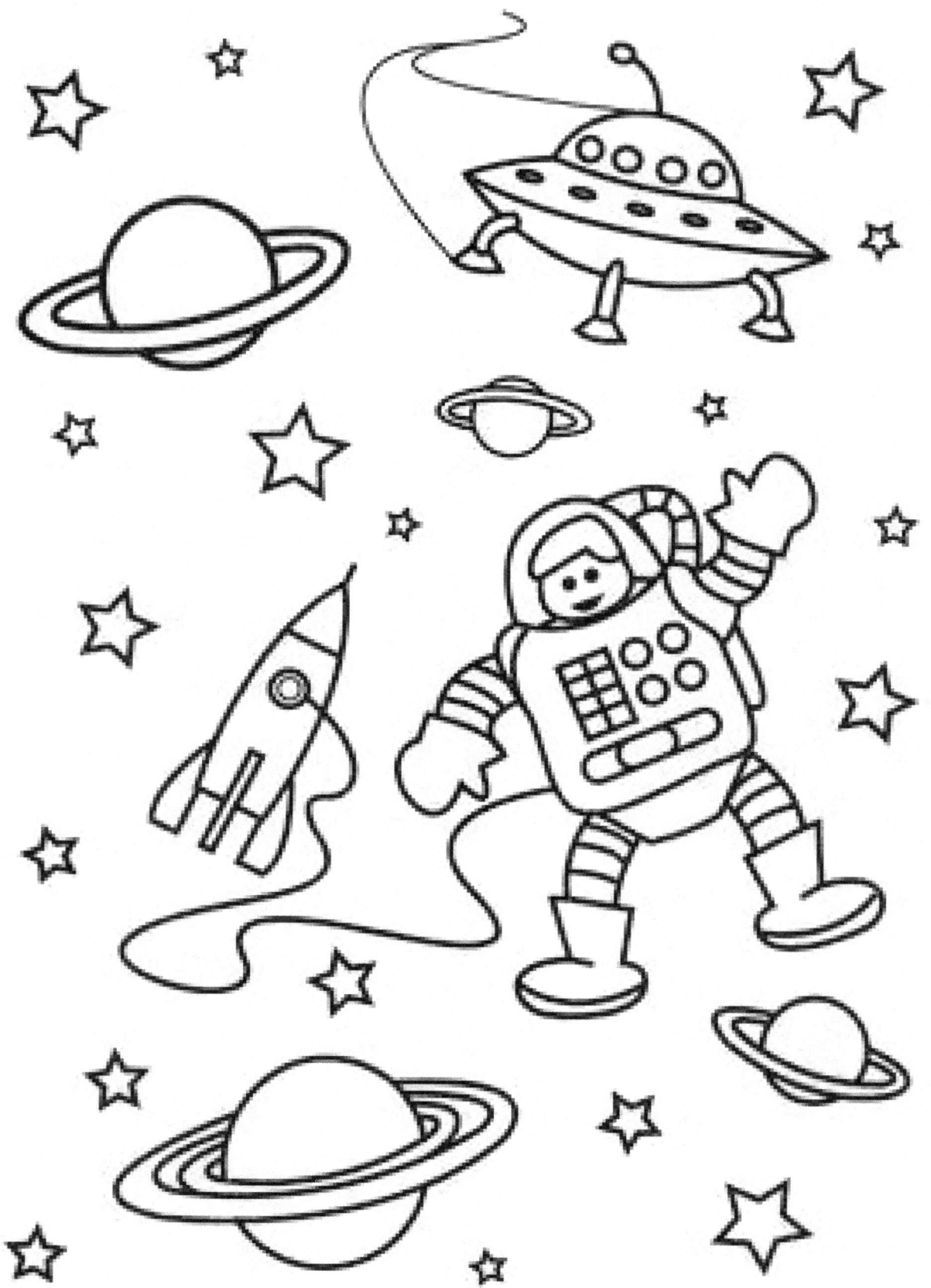

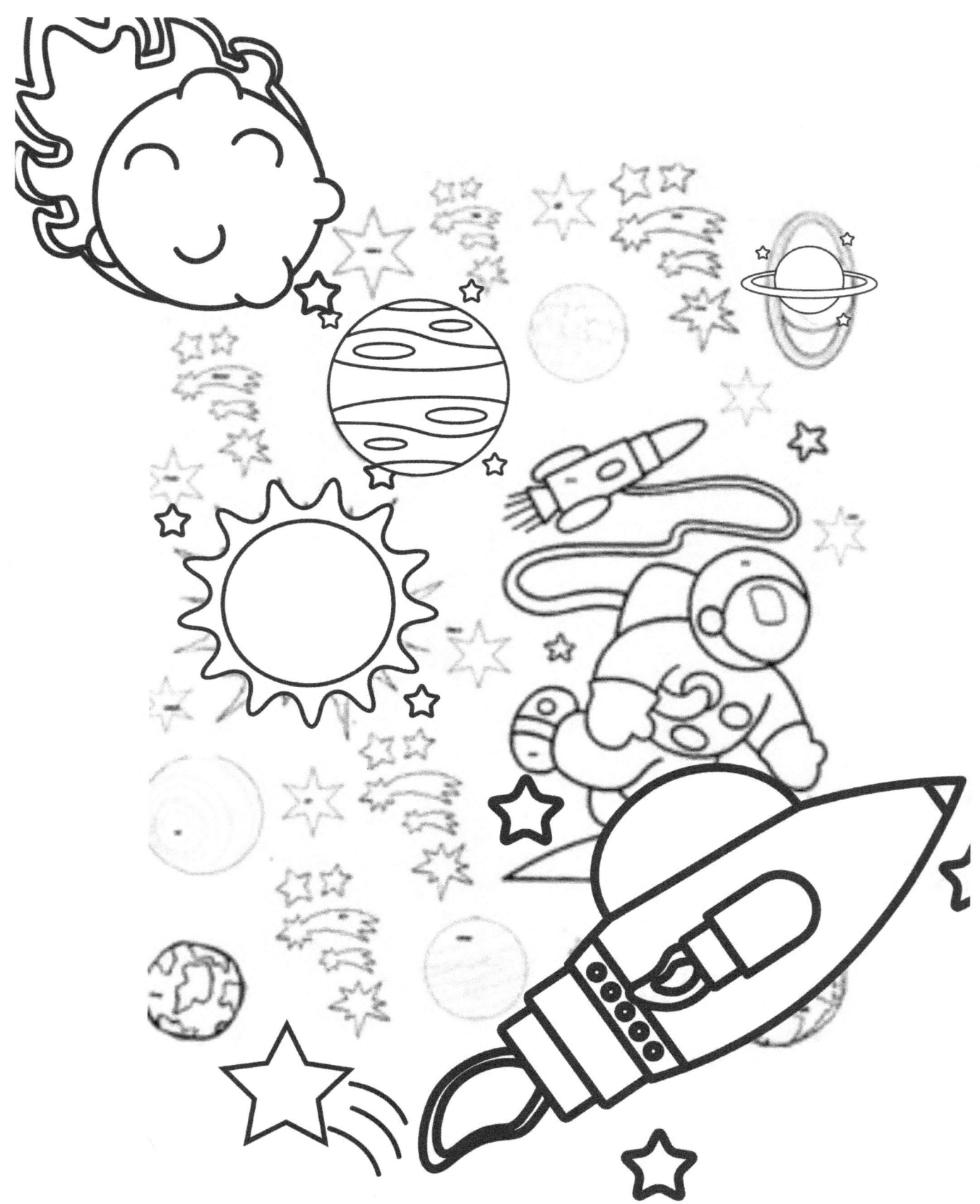

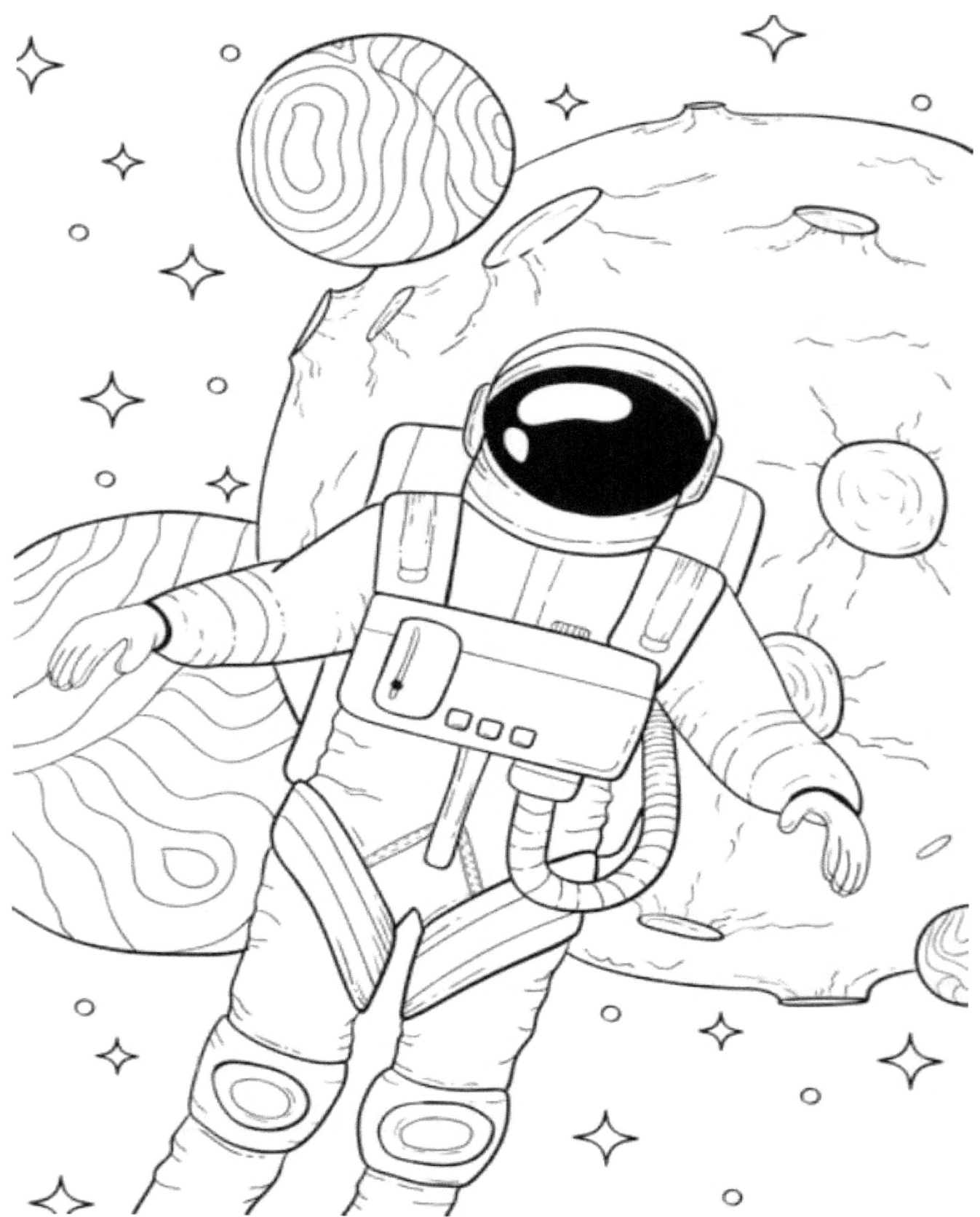

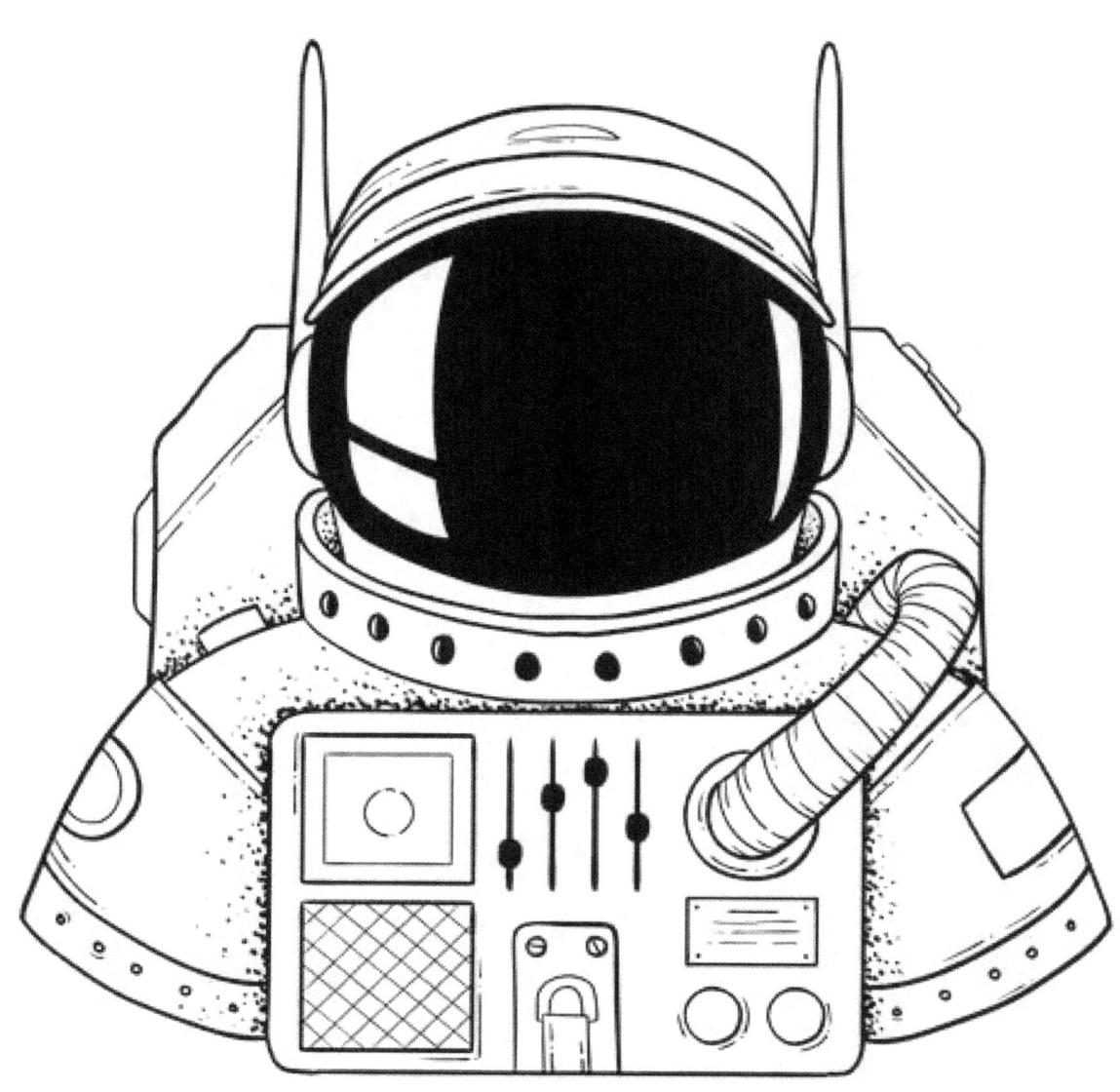

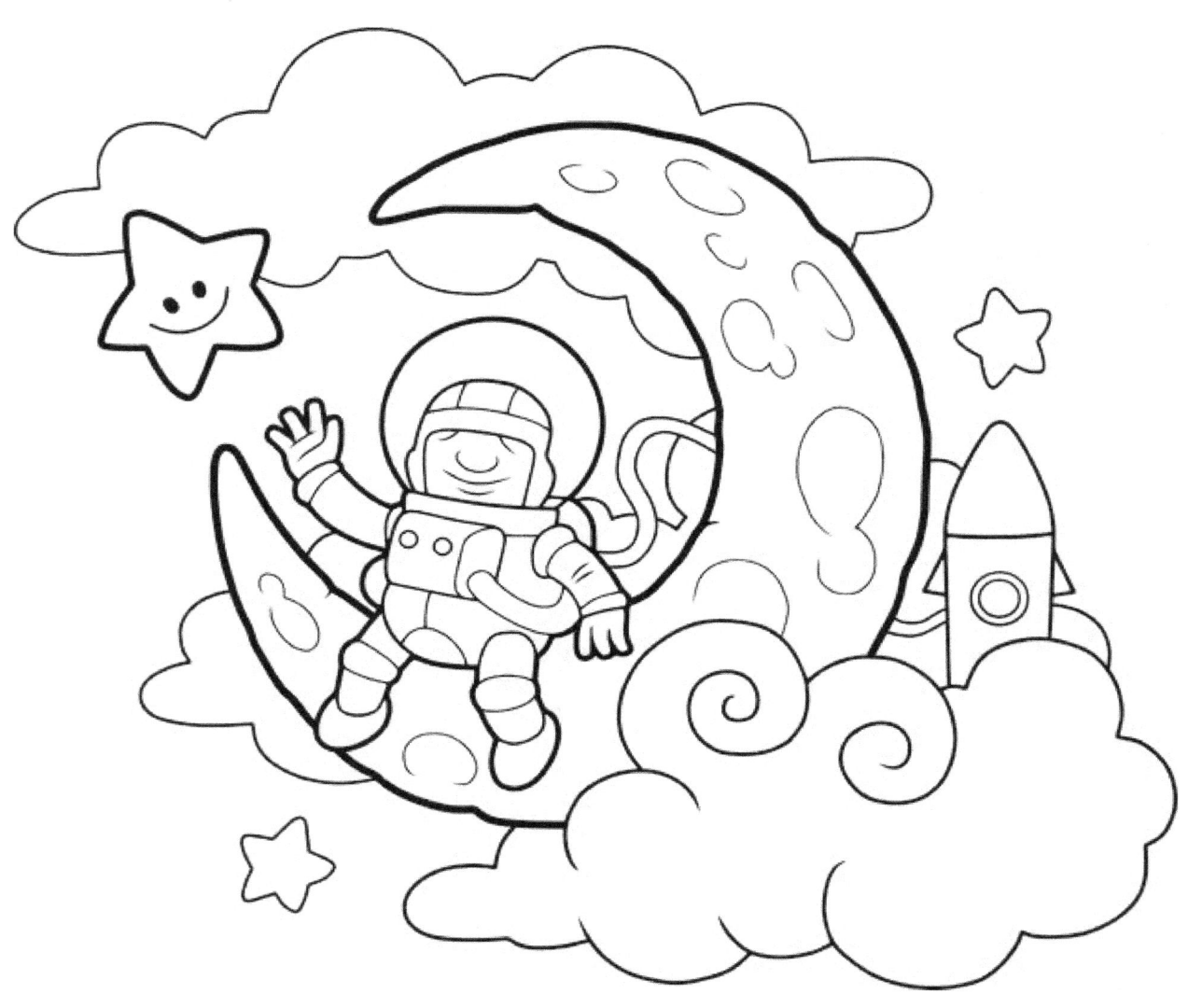

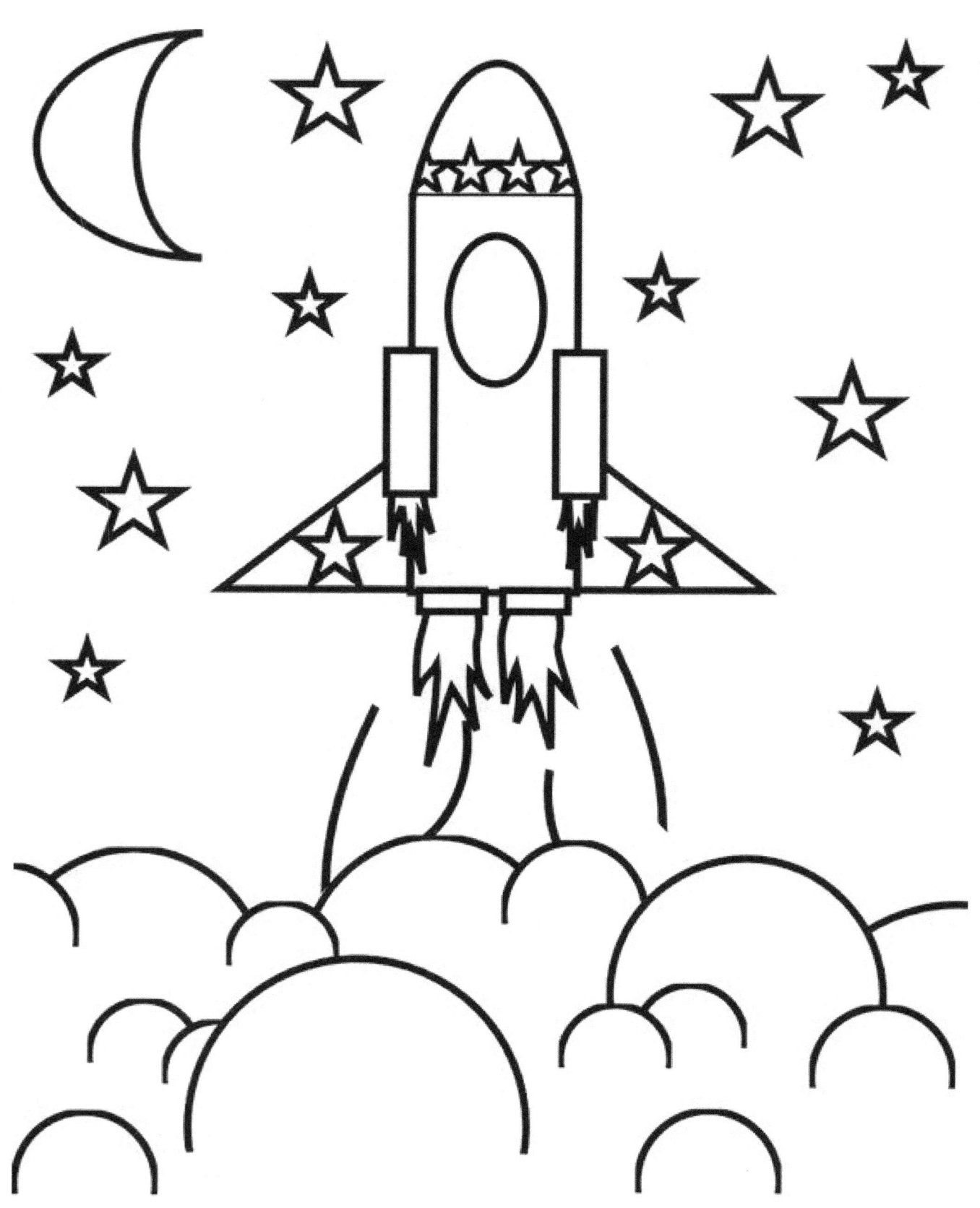

www.ingramcontent.com/pod-product-compliance
Lightning Source LLC
Chambersburg PA
CBHW080614220526
45466CB00010B/3340